CONTENTS

Fact Files 6-17

1 Bhang! 19

2 Jungle Clinic 27

3 Hot Stories 37

4 Maradadi 41

5 Money Trap 47

6 Down Grade 53

7 The Grub 59

8 Fly Fighting 67

9 Trouble in the Wind 77

10 Strike and Break-in 85

11 Whirlwind 93

12 Epidemic 99

13 Hospital! Urgent! 109

14 Second-hand Water 117

15 Night Duty 125

16 Scientific Charm 131

17 Gates 141

18 Cramp 147

19 Ominous Night 153

20 Reaping The Whirlwind 159

Sample Chapter 168-173

Fact File: Paul White

Born in 1910 in Bowral, New South Wales, Australia, Paul had Africa in his blood for as long as he could remember. His father captured his imagination with stories of his experiences in the Boer War which left an indelible impression. His father died of meningitis in army camp in 1915, and he was left an only child without his father at five years of age. He inherited his father's storytelling gift along with a mischievous sense of humour.

He committed his life to Christ as a sixteen-year-old school-boy and studied medicine as the next step towards missionary work in Africa. Paul and his wife, Mary, left Sydney, with their small son, David, for Tanganyika in 1938. He always thought of this as his life's work but Mary's severe illness forced their early return to Sydney in 1941. Their daughter, Rosemary, was born while they were overseas.

Within weeks of landing in Sydney, Paul was invited to begin a weekly radio broadcast which spread throughout Australia as the Jungle Doctor Broadcasts - the last of these was aired in 1985. The weekly scripts for these programmes became the raw material for the Jungle Doctor hospital stories - a series of twenty books.

Paul always said he preferred life to be a 'mixed grill' and so it was: writing, working as a Rheumatologist, public speaking, involvement with many Christian organisations, adapting the fable stories into multiple

JUNGLE DOCTOR
and the Whirlwind

①

JUNGLE DOCTOR
and the Whirlwind

Paul White

CF4·K

10 9 8 7 6 5 4 3 2

Jungle Doctor and the Whirlwind ISBN 978-1-84550-296-6
© Copyright 1987 Paul White
First published 1952. Reprinted 1953, 1955, 1956, 1958, 1961,
1963. Paperback edition 1967. Reprinted 1972,
Revised edition 1987. Reprinted 1990, 1995
by Paul White Productions,
4/1-5 Busaco Road, Marsfield, NSW 2122, Australia

Published in 2007 and reprinted in 2008 by
Christian Focus Publications, Geanies House, Fearn, Tain
Ross-shire, IV20 1TW, Scotland, U.K.
Fact files: © Copyright Christian Focus Publications

Cover design: Daniel van Straaten
Cover illustration: Craig Howarth
Interior illustrations: Graham Wade
Printed and bound in Denmark by Norhaven A/S

*Since the Jungle Doctor books were first published there have been a
number of Jungle Doctors working in Mvumi Hospital, Tanzania, East
Africa - some Australian, some British, a West Indian and a number of
East African Jungle Doctors to name but a few.*

African words are used throughout the book, but explained at least once
within the text. A glossary of the more important words is included at
the front of the book along with a key character index.

forms (comic books, audio cassettes, filmstrips), radio and television, and sharing his love of birds with others by producing bird song cassettes - and much more...

The books in part or whole have been translated into 107 languages.

Paul saw that although his plan to work in Africa for life was turned on its head, in God's better planning he was able to reach more people by coming home than by staying. It was a great joy to meet people over the years who told him they were on their way overseas to work in mission because of the books.

Paul's wife, Mary, died after a long illness in 1970. He married Ruth and they had the joy of working together on many new projects. He died in 1992 but the stories and fables continue to attract an enthusiastic readership of all ages.

Fact file: Tanzania

The Jungle Doctor books are based on Paul White's missionary experiences in Tanzania. Today many countries in Africa have gained their independence. This has resulted in a series of name changes. Tanganyika is one such country that has now changed its name to Tanzania.

The name Tanganyika is no longer used formally for the territory. Instead the name Tanganyika is used almost exclusively to mean the lake.

During World War I what was then Tanganyika came under British military rule. On December 9, 1961 it became independent. In 1964, it joined with the islands of Zanzibar to form the United Republic of Tanganyika and Zanzibar, changed later in the year to the United Republic of Tanzania.

It is not only its name that has changed. This area of Africa has gone through many changes since the Jungle Doctor books were first written. Africa itself has changed. Many of the same diseases raise their heads, but treatments have advanced. However new diseases come to take their place and the work goes on.

Missions throughout Africa are often now run by African Christians and not solely by foreign nationals. There are still the same problems to overcome however. The message of the gospel thankfully never changes and brings hope to those who listen and obey. *The Jungle Doctor* books are about this work to bring health and wellbeing to Africa as well as the good news of Jesus Christ and salvation.

Fact File: Dysentery

Dysentery is not a disease but a symptom of a potentially deadly illness. The term refers to infectious diarrhoea. It kills as many as 700,000 people worldwide every year.

Dysentery is the body's response to parasites or bacteria in the digestive system. Epidemics can sweep through entire cities, or regions.

Bacteria that cause dysentery often thrive in food and water that has been contaminated by human faeces and sewage. Fruits and vegetables that are grown with contaminated water can also be a common source of disease. The infection can spread rapidly through households when people don't wash their hands after using the bathroom, or before handling food.

People infected with dysentery suffer from diarrhoea, fever, intense stomach pains and rapid weight loss. Cramps are also common.

Effective treatment often starts with giving the patient a rehydrating solution, that is water mixed with salt and carbohydrates.

Nowadays antibiotics may be prescribed. Unfortunately, some bacteria are becoming resistant to common antibiotics, and effective medicine is often in short supply in developing countries.

Good hygiene is most important in avoiding dysentery. Very often the only safe thing to drink is boiled water. Food can also harbour infectious bacteria. Salads, uncooked fruits and vegetables are just some of the problem areas.

Fact File: Dysentery

Dysentery is not a disease but a symptom of a potentially dangerous illness. The term refers to infectious diarrhoea. It kills as many as 700,000 people worldwide every year.

Dysentery is the body's response to parasites or bacteria in the digestive system. Epidemics can sweep through waste clutes or...

It means that things may often thrive in food and that ... transferred by human faeces ... ... grown with ... common source ... spread mostly through faeces when people don't wash their hands after using the bathroom.

Diseases carried with ... include cholera. Being pregnant ... cramps and weight loss/ cramps are also common.

Effective treatment starts with giving the patient a rehydrating solution that is water mixed with salt and carbohydrates.

Nowadays antibiotics may be prescribed. Unfortunately, some bacteria are becoming resistant to certain antibiotics and effective medicine is often in short supply in developing countries.

Good hygiene is most important in avoiding dysentery. Very often the only safe thing to drink is boiled water. Food can also harbour infectious bacteria. Unwashed, uncooked fruits and vegetables are just some of the problem areas.

Fact File: Malaria

In Africa, a child dies from malaria every thirty seconds. Malaria is an infectious disease that kills between one and three million people every year. Most of these deaths occur with young children in Sub-Saharan Africa.

When a mosquito bites, a small amount of blood is taken in which contains microscopic malaria parasites. These grow and mature in the mosquito's gut for a week or more, then travel to the salivary glands. When the mosquito next takes a blood meal, these parasites mix with the saliva and are injected into the bite.

The parasites grow and multiply in the liver and it can take as little as eight days or as long as several months before the parasites enter the red blood cells. After they mature, the infected red blood cells rupture, freeing the parasites to attack other red blood cells. Toxins released when the red cells burst cause the typical fever, chills, and flu-like malaria symptoms.

Malaria can be reduced by preventing mosquito bites with mosquito nets and insect repellents. Spraying insecticides inside houses and draining standing water where mosquitoes lay their eggs are two ways of controlling the disease.

No vaccine is currently available; preventative drugs must be taken continuously to reduce the risk of infection but these are often too expensive for people living in the third world. Malaria infections are treated through the use of drugs, such as quinine. However, drug resistance is increasingly common.

Fact File: Characters

Let's find out a bit about the people in the story before we start. Bwana is the Chief Doctor at the hospital and the key character. He's the one who is often telling the stories as they happen - and is also known as The Jungle Doctor. Daudi is his deputee or assistant. There are a lot of others working at the hospital too such as Yakobo and Sechelela. There are school staff and other characters as well. Take a moment or two now to familiarise yourself with their names.

HOSPITAL STAFF:

Bwana – Chief Doctor
Daudi – Deputee/assistant
Yakobo - Deputee/assistant when Daudi leaves
Sechelela – Senior nurse
Hewa - staff nurse
Mwendwa - staff nurse
Hefsi - nurse
Pepetua - nurse
Marita - nurse on maternity ward
Sala - trained nurse
Yona - Sala's husband
Mboga - hospital worker also known as Spinach
Other hospital staff: Mbu, Kalama, Ngoma

SCHOOL STAFF:

Perisi – teacher and nurse
Bibi - name given to both head nurse and head teacher

OTHER STAFF:

Elisha - carpenter
Samson – handyman
Mhano - water carrier
Jason Malenga - mason
Pastor Daniel - local pastor

OTHER CHARACTERS:

Maradadi - villain
Mfupi - young boy/helper
Pungu - young boy
Nhonya - young girl patient
Mzee - Old man from Bogolo
Mwanda - young girl/patient
Baruti - the hunter

Fact File: Words

EXPRESSIONS THAT ADD EMPHASIS:
Eeeeh; Eheh; Heeeh; Hongo; Kah; Koh; Kumbe; Yoh

DIFFERENT SENTENCES AND THEIR MEANINGS:
Mpumbafu Nye! - You stupid muddlehead!
Nda yangu yikuluma - Behold, my stomach bites.
Nda yangu yikuzumha - Behold, my stomach jumps.
Tumekwisha kufanya striki - We have gone on strike.
Nghwiguta - I have no more room.
Mukubita hayi - Where are you going?
Fanya kazi! – Get on with the job!

WORDS IN ALPHABETICAL ORDER:

Askaris – Police officers
Bhang – hash-hish!'
Bibi – grandmother
Bwana – male name of respect
Chisima – the well
Dudu – insect; mosquito
Fundis – experts
Habari – what news is there
Heya – yes
Ifulafumbi – the whirlwind
Ihowe – the crow
Ivunde– the wind
Karibu – welcome
Kaya – house
Kitabu – the book
Kwaheri – goodbye

Bakuli – a dish
Basi! – that's the end of it!'
Bomba – insecticide spray.
Chambuzi – profit
Debes – containers
Fez – hat
Gazetti – local newspaper
Hatari – danger
Hodi – may I come in?'
Ihazi – the fly
Ilimba – instrument
Kanzu – long garment
Kasuku - parrot
Kifaru – rhino
Knobkerries – knobbed sticks
Lusona – congratulations

16

Lwivi – the chameleon

Mahazi – flies

Mapepo – spirits

Mbwuka - greetings

Mhungo – fever

Muganga – witchdoctor

Mugogo – a local Gogo tribesman

Mwanda – the slave

Ng'o – No

Ondoka – clear out

Serikali – the soldiers

Shauri – discussion

Sukuma - push

Ugali – millet porridge

Wachristo - the Christians

Wakali – fierce ones

Wandugu – friends/relations

Magu - I don't know

Manumit – an evil one

Mbisi – the hyaena

Miti miswanu – good medicines

Mjinga – a fool

Mzungu – a European

Njee – the scorpion

Pima – examine

Shaitan – the devil

Sindano – the needle

Tayari sasa –ready now

Vidudu – germs or parasites

Waganga – witchdoctors

Wasugu – the cunning ones

Yayagwe – Oh, my mother

TANZANIAN LANGUAGES:

Swahili (main language)

Chigogo (one of the 150 tribal languages)

1
Bhang!

'That's *bhang, hash-hish*!' Mboga shouted to make himself heard above the clatter of the railway yard. 'It's an evil medicine that makes some people as mad as a charging rhino and others too stupid to move off an ants' nest.'

We were standing near the railway station at Dodoma in Tanzania along a path that was some twenty paces from the metre-gauge track which led from the East African coast to the Great Lakes. A large African police sergeant marched a gaudily dressed young man of the local tribe. The prisoner was frothing at the mouth and yelling at the top of his voice.

The whistle of a goods train sounded long and shrill. The policeman glanced over his shoulder and in that second was tripped by the frenzied man who dragged his arm free and dashed across the rails almost under the wheels of the engine.

The driver yelled, '*Mpumbafu Nye!* You stupid muddle head!'

The irate sergeant stood with his hands on his hips. To attempt to follow was hopeless. There were thirty trucks in that train and by the time the guard's van had passed, his prisoner was lost in the crowded streets.

We walked across the shaded avenue of trees. The sergeant shook his head. 'Behold, he nearly became food for vultures and hyenas. Many are using this marijuana these days. We will certainly catch him again, but he can do all sorts of damage in the meantime.'

'Is it not possible to destroy the gardens of those who grow this Indian hemp plant?' I asked.

The big policeman shrugged his shoulders. 'To grow is not forbidden by the law.'

'*Kah!*' grinned Mboga. 'So he and those like him smoke their cigarettes, snuff their snuff, lose their wisdom and give much trouble to you and to the other *askaris*.'

The sergeant nodded. 'And they can bring difficult work to you at the hospital. Are you on safari, Bwana doctor?'

'Yes, and we're nearly finished. We're visiting small hospitals, giving out medicine in villages way out in the bush and finding those who need to come into hospital for operations on their eyes.'

'And your helper is this man of many words, Mboga?' I nodded. 'Travel with special care. There is trouble about these days since they prepare to grow many peanuts in the fertile country below the hills near Kongwa.'

'What kind of trouble, Bwana sergeant?'

He shook his head. 'Many who are *fundis* - experts - at taking what isn't their own are about. They come from all over the land and even from Kenya. They will steal anything they think they can sell - even the wheels from your car.'

Mboga laughed. 'There is small profit in the wheels of Sukuma.'

I explained. '*Sukuma* in Swahili means "push" and that is the best way to start her. See, is she not waiting for us on a slope?'

'*Heeeh.*' Mboga's eyes twinkled. 'This we find the easiest way to wake her from sleep.'

As we opened the doors of the veteran Ford the *askari* saluted. '*Kwaheri* - goodbye - may your safari be successful.'

Sukuma coughed and sputtered and then moved sedately away from the township. We shuddered our way along the corrugated gravel road leaving behind us a cloud of fine dust.

Soon we were driving through thorn bush country dotted every now and then with small hills of piled-up granite boulders. In places there were patches of dried stalks of maize and millet.

Mboga pointed with his chin. 'Where the soil is good they plant. These last two years the rains have been good. They started in November and went through to March. The harvest was excellent. This year I fear it will be different. I fear for the peanut planters.'

Lorry after lorry came towards us almost smothering us with red, powdery dust. '*Kumbe*! They pay much money to those who drive trucks these days.' A wistful note came into Mboga's voice. 'I wish I had much money, but a second-year male nurse receives few shillings for much work.'

I changed from Swahili into English. 'Listen, Spinach, it is a wise saying that enough is enough.'

He nodded and went on in Swahili. 'I understand you, but many think your words have small value and that your proverb is of the same sort. At the peanut growing there is money for those who want it and have cunning in their heads. *Kumbe*! There are many who love money.' He paused and spoke slowly and with emphasis, 'And I am one of them.'

We drove along in silence for a while. I avoided the larger potholes and accelerated when we came to a long downhill stretch. With Sukuma going as fast as she knew how, we jolted less and entered into a patch of thorn bush jungle. 'Tell me, Spinach, is this a piece of country where there are rhinos?'

He nodded vigorously. 'And there are those that trap them in a way that would bring you no joy. They make a big loop in a strong piece of wire and put it along the paths that the great animals travel to a water hole. *Kifaru* blunders along and pokes his head into the loop.' Mboga turned towards me and acted out the scene. 'It tightens. He struggles. It cuts into him. He battles. He runs this way. He runs that and the wire cuts in deeper and deeper. He is frantic with pain but all his efforts are useless. Perhaps for a day or longer he struggles and then he dies. Then comes the trapper, hacks the great horn from the bridge of the dead beast's nose and sells it to one of the traders and makes much money.'

'And the trader makes a lot more money, I suppose. But what of the rhino?'

'Food for hyaenas and vultures and thousands of flies and ants.'

'How would you like to be caught in a trap like that, Mboga?'

He shook his head. 'It is a thing of no joy.'

'You mean to say that if you saw a trap you would not walk into it?'

He laughed. 'Do you think I'm stupid, Bwana doctor?'

'I hope not. *Kah*! How I hope not.'

We turned off from the main road and drove between great grey boulders over a wide stretch of red earth. Occasional cacti stuck out their spikes. Crows flew overhead to roost in a grove of baobab trees. Abruptly the wheel was almost wrenched from my hands. We skidded wildly and pulled up against a thorn tree, its limbs weighed down with weaver birds' nests.

Mboga sighed. 'There is small joy in punctures. Let us mend this one with speed and skill or there will be no answer for the famine that calls within me.' He used a trick he had learned from Samson, our hospital strong man, and lifted the whole of the left side of the car off the ground while I slipped the jack into place. He grunted and started to unscrew the punctured wheel.

I lay at full length under the old box-bodied Ford. I could see Tanzania from an unusual angle. In front lay the apology for a road. Framed between the front wheels was a typical picture of the thorn bush savanna country: a squat Gogo house - mud-and-wattle walled with a bundle of grass and some pumpkins on the flat roof, and beyond it a boy armed with a knobbed stick was driving a few hungry-looking hump-backed cattle and an assortment of goats and fat-tailed sheep.

Mboga levered off the tyre, blew up the punctured tube and placed it on a patch of dust. A small crater in the dust showed us where the puncture was. He marked it quickly and ran his hand round inside the tyre cover. Using an old pair of dental forceps he drew out a five-centimetre long thorn. Ten minutes later we were on safari again. Mboga was handling the thorn thoughtfully.

'It's hard, sharp, difficult to see, and the cause of all our trouble.'

I nodded. 'In a way it's a trap too.'

24

'Trap?' questioned Mboga. 'You're talking a lot about traps this afternoon.'

'You started it. You said, "I wish I had much money. I love money."'

'Well, why not, Bwana? If you have money you can buy things.'

'Spinach, my friend, you do not understand. Would Rhino have put his head into the noose if he'd seen it? Would I have driven over that thorn if I had seen it sticking up in the dust? This is the cunning of traps. Animals and people don't realise they're there.'

'*Yoh*, when you call me Spinach I know you have something you want me to remember.'

'It's what your name means in English and I like the sound of it.'

We drove over a dry riverbed and up the steep bank on the far side. Ahead of us was a hospital where we would work for a few days. People ran out to greet us.

'Make sure you deal properly with your famine,' I laughed, 'for we will be busy tomorrow. I will have many injections to give and you will have the chance to show your skill in bandaging. Oh, and, Mboga, would you see if Elisha has finished his building? Ask him to be ready to return with us in two days' time.'

2
Jungle Clinic

Mboga was all smiles. 'Last village of our safari, last day of our safari. Tonight, Bwana doctor, we shall be home at Mvumi.'

We had set up a clinic under a shady umbrella-shaped thorn tree. There was a large and a small table and half-a-dozen three-legged stools. Coming towards us were three nurses, one with a kerosene tin full of water balanced on her head. The second had a basket loaded with bandages, splints and a variety of medical instruments. Behind them came the bush hospital staff nurse, Mwendwa - on her head a box loaded with large bottles full of medicines, each of a different colour, and a somewhat battered kettle.

Mboga helped her unload these. '*Yoh*,' he informed all near enough to hear his cheerful voice, 'where would we be if there were no *debes*.' He tapped the kerosene tin with his foot and used his hands dramatically. 'Behold it stores water and, cut in this way it is a dish, in that way - it's a tray. Cut it with skill and use solder

and you have a funnel, flatten it out and it's part of your roof or you door.' He lifted a primus stove from the basket. 'And what comes in *debes* gives us light and it's food for this small stove.'

'You speak truly,' nodded Mwendwa. 'And we have a fire without trouble. Truly, he was a man of wisdom who first made these.' She arranged the colourful row of large bottles and beside them put a tray of lids from tomato sauce bottles which were our version of medicine glasses.

A crowd of people had already arrived and were sitting in the shade watching all that was happening. There was an undercurrent of whispering and a variety of noises of amazement with a background of coughs, muffled groans and babies crying.

An old man with elaborate ear ornaments limped up to me and greeted me in the traditional fashion, asking after my sleep, my health, my appetite, the condition of my garden, my cattle and the welfare of my wife and children. Before I could finish all the answers he stretched out his hands to the coloured bottles of medicine. '*Miti miswanu* - good medicines. I know them well. Brown for coughs. Black for blood. Blue for those whose kidneys have no strength and *yoh*! The white medicine, it brings peace to the troubled stomach and silences the voice of the snakes that hiss and gurgle within.'

'Many have come to drink our medicine so let us start. First, though, let us ask God to be with us and thank Jesus for giving us life for our souls.' There was silence as Mwendwa prayed.

'Now, everybody who has coughs or pains in the chest.'

Almost half of those who waited surged forward. Mwendwa came to me with the kettle. I held my right hand above my left and she poured water over them. She had bucket underneath to catch any water that spilled. Smilingly, she said, 'Water is what we need most. I will use this on my small garden which gives me tomatoes and paw-paws in the dry season.'

My first patient was a young woman with a baby on her back. She swung the baby down and pointed to my stethoscope. I listened. The baby coughed but his trouble was only in the throat. I caught a satisfying glimpse of a very red throat.

'I, too, have the trouble,' said the mother.

'Do what the child did,' answered Mwendwa. 'Open your mouth wide as a hippo.' I had a magnificent view. I listened to her chest.

'What do your ears tell you about me, Bwana?'

'They say "a big measure of brown medicine for you and a small measure for your child."'

Again and again I went through the routine and the level in the brown medicine bottle became lower and lower. At last Mboga said, 'Bwana doctor, coughs are finished. Shall I...?' He placed his hands over the buckle of his belt.

I nodded. He called out, 'Now for those who have small joy in their stomachs.'

For an hour I listened to a list of sad stories, each with a full explanation of the cause. These were both imaginative and dramatic. To a large number of these people not only was the white medicine given but when I nodded to Mbu and Kalama, they smiled and worked enthusiastically with their purple medicine, their Globur Salts (which was produced in Tanzania) and their bran.

While all this was going on, Mboga worked busily with a thermometer and a yellow crayon. All who complained of *mhungo* - fever - had their temperatures taken. He put what was called 'the glass nail' under the sick person's arm. 'Safer to do it here, Bwana. There are less teeth.'

He ran his hand over skin below the ribs on each side. The yellow crayon traced out enlarged spleens or livers.

In the extreme heat of midday the kettle changed its job from a supply of water for hand washing to filling a large teapot. Mwendwa had cooked *ugali* - millet porridge - and young Kalama proudly produced a paw-paw the size of a football.

A drop of blood had been taken from all whose temperature was raised and for the best part of an hour I examined blood slides for the minute purple circles amongst the pink peach-petal-like red blood cells which signposted malaria.

I looked up from the microscope. On the paper in front of me were ten names. We handed out pills to four of these. The others had heavy infections of Africa's greatest killer. People crowded round to witness the drama of injection. The six sat poised over a form. Mboga slapped himself in the area of his hip pocket. The sick people did what was necessary in adjusting their clothing.

'I have no fear of the tooth of *sindano* - the needle,' loudly announced a boy who had shown no trouble in his blood.

Mboga made a grab at him. 'Prove it,' he shouted.

The boy bolted off towards the village followed by shouts of laughter.

Rapidly I injected quinine. As I rubbed the place where the needle had entered the last sick man, Elisha, the carpenter limped towards us down the rough track. He carried a bag of tools over his shoulder. He called a greeting and pointed excitedly with his chin towards the hills.

I looked up from re-sterilising syringes and needles and saw people shouting and scurrying off to their mud-and-wattle houses in the nearby villages. Mwendwa and her helpers hastily gathered up medicines and equipment while Mboga urged, 'Bwana. Do not do that work yet. Look at that tribe of angry clouds above the hills. Soon there will be winds of great strength and dust - choking dust and *ifulafumbi* - the whirlwinds, will tear their way through the country. Will they not do more damage than a herd of wild elephants?'

Elisha loaded his bag into the back of Sukuma. 'He's right. There will be wind storms but no rain. This will be a year of famine. The rains will fail and those who plan to grow peanuts at Kongwa will have sadness. Their digging will be in vain, their planting fruitless.'

Hastily we packed the medical equipment and waved goodbye as we drove past the hospital. The vast black clouds swept down and swallowed up the sun. Gloom closed in. Sand and stones peppered us and rattled against the windscreen. It was all I could do to keep Sukuma on the track. We crashed through thorn bush scrub. Thump! A lump of granite the size of a coconut cannoned into the door beside me. Over the hill snaked a whirlwind shaped like a huge funnel. It roared across the plains like an express train.

Elisha ran his tongue over his teeth and spat out dust and grit. '*Koh*! We have only tasted the breath of that angry wind. See, it has its teeth into the cornstalks of that garden. Behold, it tears up the thorn bushes as though they were thistles.'

We watched it wrench off great limbs of a baobab tree and snap a tall cactus like a carrot.

Amazed, we watched yet another whirlwind. The swirling monster staggered its destructive way through the jungle. 'That could wreck a village in a minute,' muttered Elisha.

'...or a hospital,' added Mboga. 'My bones tell me there is trouble ahead of us.'

It had been a wild half hour. There was a red haze

in the sky and the atmosphere was loaded with dust. That evening we saw a magnificent sunset.

'*Hatari*, danger,' muttered Elisha. 'When the whole sky is the colour of blood we know…'

It was well after dark when we reached the hospital. Sechelela, the head nurse, hurried towards us.

'What's the news?' I asked.

'The news is good, Bwana,' and then in true African fashion, 'but many things have gone wrong. A week ago Bibi (the Australian nurse) became ill with fever. She is still too weak to walk.' Her voice had an edge to it. 'And a pestilence has come into the thinking of some of our staff. Their mouths are full of grumbling words and when I tell them to do things they shrug their shoulders and just sit.'

An excited voice shouted, 'Seche, come quickly. A work of importance in the room where children are born.'

We hurried to the maternity ward - a ward not as tidy as it usually was. Hewa, a trained staff nurse, was the only one on duty. She looked utterly weary. For the next hour there was not a spare minute to talk. We were fighting for two lives, battling with makeshift apparatus by the light of a hurricane lantern. A mosquito buzzed near my ear.

Sechelela moved close. 'Don't move!' she ordered. 'These days are too full for you to lie in bed shivering and sweating with fever. That miserable *dudu* shall not bite you.' Her arm moved fast. The mosquito died and my ear rang.

At long last mother and child were safe - living and well. '*Lusona* - congratulations,' I said quietly, bending over the mother and her newly born baby.

'*Kumbe*!' yawned Seche. 'What a night.'

'You speak words of truth. Tell me, can you manage here, Seche?'

The old nurse nodded. 'Here, yes. But in other parts of the hospital it can be very different.'

I walked between silent wards towards the hospital gate. A husky voice came from the shadows behind me. 'Doctor.'

'Why, hullo, Daudi. I'm glad to see you, my friend. Why, everything seems to…'

Daudi interrupted. 'I seek opportunity to rest.'

My heart sank, for I knew that this meant that my senior assistant, my trusted friend and helper, was giving up his job. For a moment I was speechless.

'But, Daudi, why? What…?'

Daudi turned his back on me and walked off into the darkness.

3
Hot Stories

With weary feet I walked down the path through the dry cornstalks. Ahead was my white-washed mud-brick house with its battered corrugated iron roof.

Out of the shadows limped Elisha. Even in the middle of the night he wore his hat which looked uncommonly like an inverted flower pot with a dangling tassel.

'*Hodi* - may I come in?'

'*Karibu* - welcome.'

'Bwana, I saw your lamp and behold, my mind whirls like *ifulafumbi*. Sleep refused to come and fears like the teeth of white ants gnawed into my mind.'

I opened the door. 'Come in and we will talk.' I pumped up the primus and put on my whistling kettle.

The carpenter sighed deeply. 'It's this. The country of Ugogo where I was born, where I have lived all my life - it's changing in a way that brings me no joy. They're killing it and people's minds are being poisoned. I saw all this happening when I was in Kongwa as I nailed on the new roof at the hospital there. This fertile place at the bottom of the tall hills is being ruined. No longer do they dig with hoes but they tear the heart out of the country with those great yellow machines. They do it before the rains come and the winds blow away the best of the soil as dust.'

He shook his head and looked gloomily at his crippled left ankle. 'And people - they all talk money, money, money. It's *chambuzi* - profit - that fills their minds.'

He took of his hat and I was intrigued to see that in his red fez, tucked into the sweat band, was a foldable

rule and an assortment of nails. He chose one of these and scratched his head. 'At Kongwa they offered me much money to work there - five times as much as I get at the hospital. This attracted me - how it attracted me! I could buy... *Yoh*! How my thoughts flew.'

The kettle whistled. I made tea and poured a cup for each of us. Slowly he stirred it.

'But then came the words of the *wakali* - fierce ones - who would kill a man for a pocket full of shillings and the *wasugu* - the cunning ones - whose smooth words emptied purses and left despair and misery. These are the ones who steal cattle and goats and laugh their ugly laughter and jeer, "No man can prove that we stole his cattle for who will recognise his cow if it is a lump of meat in a pot?"'

He paused and sipped his tea. 'At night you do not go out without one of these.' He held up his knobbed stick with a shaft as long as your arm and capped with a tennis ball-sized lump of wood. 'After dark there are those who lurk in the shadows. Skulls are cracked with *knobkerries* - knobbed sticks - like these. Many are wounded. Some die. And all for their - money!' He spat out the word and gulped down his tea.

'Money is all right, Elisha. It's the love of it that's the trouble.'

He leaned forward. 'What shall we do then?'

I refilled his cup. 'Elisha, if you want to know the length of a plank or the width of a window, what do you do?' Without speaking he handed me the rule. 'You'd check it with this?' He nodded.

'And what a rule is to a carpenter the Bible is to a Christian. Jesus told those who followed him,

"Where your treasure - your wealth - is there will your heart be also." And Paul wrote to Timothy, a young man who faced this love of money business, "People who set their hearts on being wealthy are targets for temptation. They fall into one of the world's traps that can ruin and destroy their souls. The love of money leads to all kinds of evil and some, in the struggle to be rich, have lost their faith and caused themselves agony of mind."'

Slowly Elisha put his foldable rule back into its place. 'If people refuse to listen to what God says will they be punished?'

'Listen to my riddle, *fundi* carpenter. If you put a large flat stone into the fire and after a time you rake it out of the ashes, do you then sit on it?'

Elisha put his hat firmly on his head and chuckled. 'The matter is clear to me now. Only one of the smallest wisdom sits on hot stones.'

4
Maradadi

'A small girl has been bitten by a scorpion,' panted Pepetua, the nurse in charge of the children's ward. 'She screams and screams with pain.'

Seizing a tray with syringes and medicines I hurried with her to the bed where the child was writhing in agony.

Seeing Mboga I called out, 'I want your help.'

He came on the double. 'Scorpion bite,' I explained. 'It's magical what an injection of local anaesthetic will do. I want you to hold the child so that I can inject into the exact place.'

He nodded. It was a minute's work. The child quietened dramatically and whispered that she was thirsty. Pepetua supported her head and gave her a cup of water.

'I shall stay here for a few moments,' I told her, 'and we will watch that all goes well.'

Mboga was gripping my arm. 'Bwana, come over

here into the corner. I have news.' He was moving from foot to foot excitedly. 'You remember the man who was nearly cut to pieces by the wheels of the goods train?'

'I do, indeed. He was only the thickness of a goat from the wheels of that fast-moving engine.'

'My news is that he's here, that he's brought trouble with him. He has pockets full of money. He is dressed in clothes brighter than those of last night's sunset. His hat is green and he has the feathers of a parrot in the side of it. I heard him talking out there and he is boasting and saying that he'll put you in your place and that he will teach those of the hospital, lessons that they will never forget. Be careful, Bwana. He is full of cunning, that one. He talks of wealth and how to gain it without work if you know how. There are those that listen with wide open ears.'

I took the little girl's pulse. It had settled. 'Good. All goes well. It is now safe for me to go back to the other sick people in the outpatients.'

As Mboga and I went through the door I said, 'Surely this young man is baiting the trap that we talked about yesterday. I hope that none of our people are caught.'

Sechelela came out of the women's ward. She pointed with her chin. 'Bwana, look over there under the buyu tree near the gate. Look carefully at him. He is one who is as full of trouble as *njee*, the scorpion.'

He was dressed in the most bizarre clothing and was talking loudly to a group of people - some of them nurses. The corner of Sechelela's mouth turned up with disdain. 'He talks many words. Is he not a man of boastfulness? But if it stopped there it would not be so bad. *Koh*, doctor, he talks with his eyes, he…' She shook her head and seemed to be at a loss for words. Then she picked up a broom and gripped it in a way that I felt could make things extremely uncomfortable for that young man if he came within range.

He swaggered towards us and stopped - hands on hips, hat on head - and just looked. From the gateway I could hear a titter.

He spoke in English. 'I have money. I would purchase quinine and medicines for my own use.'

I spoke in Swahili. 'Good morning.' And then, 'How are you?' - the normal way to greet people in Tanzania.

I heard a whisper from those that stood nearby. '*Koh*! He did not greet the Bwana and behold the Bwana greets him.'

This time he stumbled out a greeting in Swahili and then said, 'I have much money. I would buy medicine. I will pay the highest prices for the medicines that you use on yourself.'

At that moment a woman pushed her way through the crowd, in her arms a baby that was only a couple of weeks old. 'Bwana,' she gasped, 'the child has the trouble which kills, even as had the daughter of Mluko. You saved her, Bwana, in the place you call operating theatre. Help my child also.'

I nodded. 'Tell me about her trouble.'

In a few words she explained what had happened and it was clear that an urgent operation must be done if the baby's life was to be saved. It was one of those uncommon happenings in which the far end of the stomach becomes closed up and the child dies from starvation because it cannot absorb anything it eats.

I was examining the child as he lay on his mother's lap. An aggressive voice behind me rasped, '*Yoh*, woman! Would you interrupt when I am talking to the Bwana?'

Anger flared up inside me. I literally saw red but that morning in the time that I spent reading the Bible and on my knees talking to God I had come across the words, 'A soft answer turns away wrath'. So crouching there, my fingers gently examining the baby's body, the thought came: long-suffering and patience are the hallmarks of those who follow God.

Slowly I got to my feet. At the back of the crowd was Daudi. I looked straight at him. 'Daudi, would you get the theatre ready, please? You, and only you, know the instruments required for this operation for pyloric stenosis.'

There was a sneer on Maradadi's face. He turned on Daudi, obviously expecting him to refuse, but my senior assistant nodded and ran down the path to the theatre. I turned to the gaudy young man. 'Listen, there are many things in life far more important than words or clothing and one of these things is the life of a child. In the next hour we will have the opportunity of saving that child's life.'

Maradadi shrugged his shoulders. '*Koh!*' He sneered at me. 'Children! They're easy enough to come by. Why make all the fuss?'

I noticed those standing round moving into groups. To some the shallowness of this self-important individual was obvious, but some of the younger ones seemed completely hypnotised by him in a way that tribal custom would frown upon.

He turned his back on me and stalked away to sit in the shade of a pomegranate tree. I hurried to the operating theatre.

This was a delicate operation which had a critical phase in the middle of it. Daudi was his usual capable deft self. Everything was prepared. I scrubbed my hands, put on gloves and before picking up the scalpel bowed my head and prayed that this small life would be saved.

Daudi was uncomfortable as we prayed. Talking to God was not a thing he relished at the moment. Hardly a word was spoken for the next twenty minutes, and then the operation came to its climax - the cutting of a small piece of tissue. A few millimetres too deep, a shade too much weight on the knife and operation would be a failure and the child would die. There was a sigh of relief from Daudi. '*Yoh*, Bwana, life hangs on so little here.'

I agreed. 'It's like making a decision, Daudi. The first step is hard and it makes all the difference to the way your journey goes.'

After a moment he said coldly, 'Bwana, I do not desire to talk of these things.'

There was silence till the last stitch was in. Sechelela picked up the baby and put him into a cot in the children's ward.

'Daudi, you may not like to talk of these things but, behold, that child did not like to undergo an operation. It had to be done, though, to save his life. You, at this time, are making a great choice. Do not turn your back on God. Do not plug your ears to his voice. God will speak to you over and over again but he never shouts. You have the right to choose your ways. God's path may be uphill, may be rough, but it leads to life, to usefulness, to contentment. The other track in front of you may be soft to the feet and lead smoothly, slightly downhill, but the end of this road is misery and death.'

He said nothing but slowly nodded his head. I could see his eyes looking through the window of the theatre. Outside was Maradadi beckoning to him. My friend's life was at the crossroads.

5

Money Trap

The surgical instruments we had been using were boiling in a steriliser on the primus stove. Daudi was standing looking out of the window, his eyes fixed on Maradadi. He undid the tapes that held the gauze mask over his mouth. I could see his whole face in profile.

Slowly he turned. 'Bwana, I have come back to the hospital to collect my wages and the money that I've put away in the savings account.'

This was no time for arguing. One thing was obvious: Daudi was acutely miserable.

'Come up with me now and I will get the money.'

As we walked out of the operating theatre we almost stumbled over a lad sitting on the step wrapped in a blanket shivering, his teeth rattling although he was sitting in bright sunlight.

'Malaria,' grunted Daudi. '*Koh*! Mosquitoes are a menace.'

'How do you know he's got malaria, Daudi?'

A slow smile came over his face. 'First, the symptoms. They stick out like the ears of a donkey. He shivers on a hot day. He perspires.' He pushed the blanket aside and ran his fingers over the boy's abdomen. 'His spleen. Look at it. It's as big as a pumpkin and the signs…our microscope will tell us the whole story.'

I helped the boy to his feet. 'Come with us. We'll take a drop of your blood and look for the *vidudu* - the little creatures that grow on the nose of mosquito. When he bites they get inside you and they breed with great speed - faster than rats. They feed upon your blood and thus you have fever and sickness and misery. *Heeeh*, we know the cause of the trouble and we have the answer.'

In our pathology room I collected a drop of blood and put it on a glass slide.

'*Hongo*, Bwana,' said Daudi. 'Let me do this while you go and count out the money.'

He stained the thin film of blood and put it under the microscope. The boy sat shivering in the corner. I counted out the money that was Daudi's and put it in a paper bag. Suddenly my attention was taken by a gaudy yellow shirt which appeared and disappeared around the corner. Then I saw its owner. It was Maradadi. He peered this way and that. I saw him poke a folded piece of paper under a clay cooking pot then, furtively, he walked in the other direction and slouched through the door of the outpatients' room as though coming in for an afternoon dose of medicine.

Back in the pathology room Daudi looked up from the microscope. 'Doctor, I was right. See these.'

I looked down the microscope and saw scores of tiny red circular affairs. In some were little purple rings. It was a typical picture of malaria.

Daudi was smiling. 'I was right, Bwana. I recognised the symptoms and the signs.

'*Eheh*, then you had a look at his blood and there was no doubt about it.'

He wiped the oil off the lens and put the microscope back in its box. I handed him the bag of money.

'Daudi, you recognised malaria because of its symptoms. Behold, do I not realise that you, too, are suffering from a disease that produces symptoms that stick out like the ears of a donkey, as you say. Now, your trouble is being self-centred. You are in the middle of your thinking and you've turned your back on God.'

He glared at me aggressively. The twinkle had gone from his eye. There was a harshness in his voice. 'Who have you been talking to? Who has told you these words?'

'Was it necessary for us to be told that that child had been bitten by a mosquito and had malarial fever? Did we need to be told? Was it not obvious to us both that he had malaria? Was it not plain? Did not the child tell us the whole story by what he looked like? Do you not tell the whole story by how you look - the look in your eye, the droop of your shoulders, even your walk?'

Daudi pushed the bag of money into his pocket. '*Kwaheri*. I am going now.'

I gave the sick boy two pills and a gourd full of water. 'Swallow those and keep close to the hospital till the evening.' He nodded.

I put out my hand to Daudi. He shook it and we stood at the door together. We could see right over the plains of East Africa stretching up towards the equator and Mount Kilimanjaro. I noticed the dry cornstalks waving in the slight breeze of late afternoon. 'Daudi, once on a day like this Abraham and Lot, his relation, stood looking from the side of a hill over plains as we are now. There had been trouble between their herdsmen and they had decided to part. Abraham said, "Choose which way you will go." Lot, the younger man, looked. He saw the plains rich and green with grass. Fine grazing for a river ran through them. It was a place for crops, for herds. But he knew it was a place where evil was common. He had heard stories of the people of the place that made his skin creep. He had heard that men turned their backs on God and rebelled against him. But then he looked up to the hill country. It was a place of rough paths, of little comfort, a place of poor crops and certainly not a place to feed herds. To cultivate there meant moving stones and digging hard earth. For a moment he stood making his choice, then he pointed to the plains and in making that choice he lost everything. Not at first, for behold, he had riches for a time and a fine house and many things that brought joy to his heart. But suddenly and unexpectedly came the other side and the end of the story was tragedy. He had made the wrong choice. He thought he'd pick the easy way but at the end he found it was bitter.'

Daudi shrugged his shoulders. 'Bwana, I'm going. I know what I want and I'll get it. It's my life and I'll live it my way.'

Just then one of the nurses, Hefsi, came to the door. 'Bwana, may I have the key of the store?'

I reached up to the nail where it hung and gave it to her and I saw a look pass between those two which was completely eloquent. To me the whole jigsaw puzzle suddenly fell into place. I watched the girl turn away with the key in her hand. Daudi gazed after her.

Softly I said, 'There was a wise one of my country who wrote these words which are cruelly true: "The sins that we sin two by two we pay for one by one". Would it not be better for both you and Hefsi to acknowledge that you've made a mess of things? You've brought open shame on Jesus who is your chief and you can't sin and get away with it. You sow one grain, remember, but you reap a harvest from your sowing.'

There was smouldering anger in Daudi's eyes. 'Enough of your words.' He swung on his heel and walked down the path past the hospital. As he went under a baobab tree I saw a yellow-shirted figure fall into step behind him. It was Maradadi. I thought again of the letter I had seen him put under the clay pot and went to see what new mischief was brewing.

6

Down Grade

I could hear the clunk, clunk, clunk of nurses pounding millet seed and their laughter and chatter as they prepared the evening meal.

Behind the kitchen was a row of large clay pots used in cooking *ugali*, the porridge which was the main food of people in this part of East Africa. Here you could feed a whole hospital cheaply. There was no call for a variety of food. If people were very sick they liked very thin porridge. If the sickness was not severe they liked it lumpy. If they were well they liked it thick. Suggest anything but porridge and they would shake their heads. '*Uhuh*. We want *ugali* - porridge.'

But I was not thinking of porridge when I examined those pots and found under one of them a folded piece of paper. I put it in my pocket and went back to my office. In good handwriting in Swahili I read: *Hefsi, greetings to you. I am well through the goodness of God. May His blessing and peace rest upon you. I trust that you too are well...*

And so it went on for at least half a page. Flowery, half-pious stuff that was little more than an excuse for covering paper with writing. But the bit I was looking for came near the end of the page. It read: *Meet me near the fence opposite the pomegranate tree when you see the lights go out in the doctor's room tonight.* It was signed: *Maradadi.*

I put the letter back into my pocket and thought that the writer would certainly meet someone when my light went out that evening but I strongly doubted that it would be Hefsi. She had been one of the most difficult members of our staff for quite some time and then, lately, there had been a change for good in her behaviour.

Sechelela, too, had noticed this and shaking her head had said, 'Doctor, I fear the hyaena most when it laughs.'

My light burned late that night. An official letter had arrived by the mail which came only once a week. I looked at the typed words which told of a rapidly spreading epidemic of dysentery carried by flies. The large parcel which had accompanied the letter contained a number of tins of pills labelled Sulphaguanidine. I read the instruction as to how these were to be used. There was a report on their usefulness in epidemics in this part of Africa.

Obviously the first step was to have an all-out drive to improve the hygiene in the villages and to wage war on flies. For half an hour I sat planning what we would do in this emergency then I remembered the flashily dressed Maradadi. He was up there in the darkness somewhere thinking of the girl in the nurses' home, looking at my window and waiting for me to turn out the lamp. I knew it was going to be an interesting evening for Maradadi.

I put on a pair of rubber-soled shoes and changed into dark blue trousers. I picked up a long sandbag which lay over the bottom of the door to keep out swirling dust. Pocketing an electric torch I put out my lamp and followed a seldom used path to the hospital. Bent double, I moved fast to take advantage of all cover possible from the dead stalks of the corn crop. Then the cover ended.

In front the path was a white line in the darkness. I went down on my hands and knees and shuffled forward setting my trap and then crawling back through the cornstalks to the shed where we kept Sukuma, the ancient truck. Opening the doors of the shed quietly I pushed Sukuma out into the darkness and, with a crowbar, manoeuvred her until I was sure that the headlights would focus sharply on the pomegranate bush where Maradadi was waiting. I flicked down the switch and the night was cut open.

A man stumbled to his feet, the gaudiness of his clothing vivid against the drabness of the night. There was no doubt that it was Maradadi. Dazzled, he dashed down the path. I kept Sukuma's spotlight on his face and tooted the horn. Suddenly he seemed to rise straight up in the air and let out a startled yell. He staggered, stumbled, partly recovered and then fell. In a twinkle he was on his feet again and bolting into the darkness. I turned out the lights and grinned. My sand-filled doorstop had looked very much like a death adder. Maradadi tripped, jumped to one side and ran for his life.

I wondered how far he could run at that speed and how long it would take for his pulse to come back to normal. Switching my torch on, I went and collected my doorstop. Near where Maradadi had stumbled was his green hat and beside it a small snuff gourd of unusual shape. I picked this up and walked back to the house where I sampled what was in the gourd. It was not tobacco snuff. A pinch of it on my tongue showed it was marijuana. This can make an ordinary person behave in extraordinary ways while disturbed people become violent and vicious. I knew only too well what happened when a little of that powder was snuffed up the nose or mixed into a cigarette. Had he been getting any of our staff onto this stuff?

It was clear to me now how Maradadi had made his money. He was a dope pedlar and had brought an infection uglier than the threat of epidemic dysentery to our hospital. Maradadi was obsessed with money and the things it can buy - things that glow with attraction at the start but end up with bitterness and brain damage.

I spent one of those nights when all sorts of weird dreams float through sleep. Waking early, I watched the tropical sunrise and prayed to God. Not long after dawn I saw Daudi standing outside my door, on his shoulder a woven basket containing most of his goods.

'Mbwuka, Daudi.'

'Mbwuka, doctor.' He spoke abruptly. 'I have chosen. Today I am going to the place where the peanuts are being grown.' He picked up his bundle and without looking back marched off down the hill.

Sadly I watched him go. He had helped me in some of the most difficult events of my life. He had stood by me in many crises, but now temptation had whispered. He had listened and chosen to play with exciting things that he knew were red hot. He would be burnt and in the burning others would be scorched. I watched him walk down the hill. It was symbolic - that down grade - of what could be ahead of him.

7
The Grub

It was with a heavy heart that morning that I walked to the hospital. The equator, five hundred kilometres north, seemed to be right over my head that day. The sun beat down mercilessly. The crows that flew overhead seemed to jeer in derision. It was going to be a difficult day to face. The head medical assistant who had been my lieutenant in the hospital for years had gone. Gone in the worst of circumstances.

This blow had come when we were facing a particularly ugly and disagreeable epidemic and were short of both staff and drugs. The staff was simmering with discontent which could and probably would be brought to a head by the disgusting nature of dysentery. There was a gleam of comfort, though. In the dispensary were sufficient pills to break the back of this ugly illness.

I sat down in the office and picked up a notebook in which I jotted down the special way the local folk described sickness and symptoms. It was a waste of time to speak learnedly of bacillary and amoebic dysentery and gastroenteritis. It was much more practical to make clear to my African helpers exactly what these words meant.

As I flicked over the pages my mind went back to when I first discovered how the Gogo people described gastritis. I was sitting one morning seeing outpatients with Daudi. An elderly woman had come in with her hands draped over her stomach. She looked unhappily at the roof and said, '*Koh*, Bwana, *nda yangu yikuluma* - behold, my stomach bites.'

I turned to Daudi, 'That means that she has gastritis?'

'Yes, that is it.'

A few minutes later a young woman had come in with her hands in the same position. She had complained, 'Bwana, *nda yangu yikuzumha* - behold, my stomach jumps.' This, Daudi informed me, was also a case of gastritis.

'But, Daudi, the other woman said her stomach bites. This one says it jumps. They can't both be gastritis.'

He chuckled. 'Doctor, in one case It was an old woman. In the other it's a young woman. This is the way we say things.'

I was not surprised when half an hour later a small boy had come in groaning and clutching his midriff. He told me that he had a restless snake within him. Daudi had smiled and said, 'This is the small boy variety of gastritis.'

I sketched out a plan of campaign on the back of

a medical journal. Dysentery was in its element in a country where sanitation was primitive or non-existent. Here flies were present in myriads and spread disease-producing germs as they pried into people's food and mouths.

Nobody bothered much to brush them away. It would take too much energy and flies were altogether too persistent. I knew that dysentery would spread through the country like flood waters unless something radical was done.

I jotted down:

1. Cover all food.

2. Keep the baby from flies and vice versa.

3. Boil all water and burn or bury deep all products of the disease.

4. Think up ways of improving sanitation as an urgent matter.

5. Inform staff and get their ideas.

At that moment Yakobo, my second-in-command, came to the door.

'*Habari*, - what news is there - Bwana?'

'The news is good, Yakobo, but we have troubles. Behold, from today on you have great responsibility. Daudi has gone, for he chooses to go to a place where there is more money to be had than in our hospital. Behold, his work will now be yours. You will now be senior assistant and you and I face a grim fight against dysentery. It comes over the plains even as the locusts do in the years when they swarm upon us. People worry about them because they helplessly watch them destroying the crops, but the *dudus* that are threatening us cannot be seen and so no one fears them. They blame witchcraft for what you and I know is the work of a germ that can only be seen under a microscope.'

He nodded quietly and we went over the plans that I had drawn up.

'Bwana, I think we can do this if only the others will work with us. But there are many words these days. They are grumbling, grumbling…and behold dysentery is a sickness which the staff detest. They have horrible jobs to do.'

'Will they do them?'

'I fear not. Amongst the girls, Hefsi for one speaks smooth words to you but in her work her ways are not the ways of God.'

I nodded. 'And I think this newcomer Maradadi has poisoned the wisdom of our friend Daudi. He has also done damage amongst the girls of the hospital. I have evidence now that he carries hash-hish, selling it or using it to mould people to do his will in the same way as a woman moulds a pot from clay.'

I took from my pocket the gourd full of hash-hish snuff. As we were looking at it a moth flew straight into my face. I clutched at it and threw it to the ground.

Yakobo put his foot on it. 'Bwana, that *dudu* is an enemy. Behold it lays its eggs on the cob of our corn when it's young. In time, as the caterpillar hatches inside the cob, though on the outside it looks green and attractive, all that remains inside is worm-eaten, sickening, an insult to the stomach. *Koh*!' There was deep disgust in his voice.

I stood up. 'Yakobo, that is exactly what I want to say to the staff this morning. This will give me a picture that they can see with their minds.'

A drum was beaten and everybody came into the outpatients' room. First we prayed together and sang a little and I read from the Bible, turning over the pages of the first book of the New Testament.

'Listen, everybody, these are Jesus' words, not mine. He said, "Do not store up riches for yourselves here on earth, where moths and rust destroy, and robbers break in and steal. Instead, store up riches for yourselves in heaven, where moths and rust cannot destroy, and robbers cannot break in and steal. For your heart will always be where your riches are. You cannot be servants both of God and of money. But put first God's kingdom and his righteousness and everyday things will be given to you as well."'

I closed the book and Yakobo jumped to his feet. 'Bwana, these words go deeply into my head. Now I understand what happens to the man who hears what Jesus says but does not obey. He is like a corn cob. Behold, it grows nicely in the stalk. Then gently, soundlessly, comes a white moth. It lays its eggs and

before long a grub hatches and eats its way to the heart of that corn cob. It eats the young corn as it grows. The green husk gives no sign of what is happening inside. And what of the grub? Does it not eat with joy in its stomach till the whole of the inside of that corn cob is a thing of no profit?'

'*Eheh*,' said Mboga, 'and you come with appetite and tear off the green covering. From the outside it looks attractive but inside, *koh*! There is nothing but rubbish and a green grub swollen with much eating. You throw the whole thing aside. The grub is food for ants.'

'True,' broke in Yakobo, 'and are we not like that? We may look all right outside but inside is the grub of sin. If you stop it at the egg stage when the moth hovers over the top you have done no wrong. No damage is done. That is only temptation. But if you let the moth settle and lay her eggs they hatch and gnaw their way inside. That's like sin.'

Elisha was leaning on the windowsill. 'You speak words of wisdom,' he said, 'and words of truth. Sin starts small and grows quickly and with it comes destruction, trouble, sadness. We have all seen it happen.'

I looked across at the staff. Some were listening, some obviously taking notice. Then Hefsi caught my eye. She was taking no interest whatsoever but was looking through the window. There was a mirror on the wall and I could see in it what was happening outside. Maradadi was sitting on a root of the baobab tree, a modern brief case held firmly between his knees.

8
Fly Fighting

Along the path to the hospital came Perisi, a trained teacher who was also a nurse. I called to her through the window of the dispensary.

'Just the person I wanted to see. Help me to come up with an idea that will save at least a hundred lives.'

'Tell me about it, Bwana,' said the smiling girl.

The threat of a dysentery epidemic was outlined in a matter of minutes. She nodded her head slowly. 'Let's teach the children that flies are more dangerous than lions. They will talk about it, their parents will hear and the elders of the tribe will talk and argue.'

'The more people that talk about it the better, Perisi, for who is frightened of a fly? They say that they're a nuisance, yes, but where are their teeth? Where are their claws? So they let the dangerous brutes cling round their eyes and their mouths while villages of germs on the flies' legs can bring suffering and misery and can kill.'

Perisi concentrated. 'This is the way to do it, Bwana. First, let us go to the girls' school...' She drew up plans in detail. Her ideas were splendid.

'This afternoon, then. There's nothing like drama to catch interest and to set imagination to work.'

I told Mboga what we planned to do. He nodded his head vigorously. 'You remember the boy, Mfupi, who had bad malaria some months back?

'Who would forget Mfupi? Laughter bubbles up from inside him.'

'It does now, Bwana, but he would have died if he had not come to hospital and been treated for his malaria. He understands about the dangers of mosquitoes. He's just the one to do the job.'

An hour later as I came out of the children's ward, there stood Mfupi. '*Mbwuka*, Bwana.'

'*Mbwuka*, Mfupi. I want your help to do something which will save many people from much sickness. You and I hate mosquitoes?' He nodded. 'Another disease threatens. This time it is flies that are our enemies. This afternoon I want you to pretend that you are *ihazi* - the fly. If flies were large as hyenas we would see the filth on their faces and legs. We would attack them and drive them from our houses and villages. But because flies are small we cannot see the danger they bring and we have no fear. If we give you wings and cover you with dirt and filth people will say, "He looks like a huge fly but *ugh*!"'

The boy giggled. 'But where will I find wings?'

'Elisha will help us.'

We walked together to the carpenter's shop and I

drew a diagram. Elisha limped to a heap of odds and ends and picked up some fencing wire and two broken broomsticks.

'You have some old bits of mosquito net in the hospital cupboard, Bwana?'

I nodded.

'Then I can do what you want. But why?'

'I want you to fit it onto Mfupi to make him look like a huge fly. We'll cover him with mud and dirty, stinking rubbish.'

The boy wriggled his nose and grinned. 'And Bwana wants me to go down to the girls' school like that and make a horrible mess.'

Elisha shook his head. 'But won't Bibi, the headmistress, down there be very angry with you?'

'No, Elisha. This will be all right. We will have a dish with food in it - some *ugali*. Mfupi will come along when he has paddled in the mud and walk over to the *ugali* in a way you can see. I want him to make shudders go up the spines of the girls so that they may know without any shadow of a doubt what flies do.'

The lame carpenter shrugged. 'I will do as you say but I do not see how it is going to help people to understand.'

Patiently, I replied, 'You need to come and see exactly what happens then you, too, will understand and you will help in the fight against flies which bring a great sickness.'

Perisi and Mboga had been hard at work. They had the old microscope that we used to train junior nurses. Mboga had caught a number of flies and mounted them on glass slides. He pointed to one slide which had a pin on it. 'They know the size of a pin, Bwana, but look at it through the microscope and, *kumbe*! You say to yourself, "Behold, it is a spear", so when they look at these flies they will shake their heads and say, ugh, ugly. Truly, they're enemies.'

'You didn't think all this up by yourself, Mboga.'

'True, doctor; Perisi had the ideas and...', he laughed, 'I saw ways of making people shudder.

Some time later Mfupi arrived with his wings in place and additional legs made from thin sticks cut from thorn trees. He carried a gourd full of water while Mboga had half a kerosene tin full of black dust and a dish full of greasy slime.

'Bwana,' said the boy, 'we will make a splendid mess. Every eye will see it. Have you not something which will speak to noses as well? I have been talking with Mboga.' He grinned impishly.

'Have you now? I'll see what I can do to bring no joy to many noses.'

Late that afternoon I had two hundred schoolgirls open-eared, listening as I told them loud and clear that a menace was marching upon Tanzania - marching in a way that produced no fear in people.

'Tell me,' I asked, 'if snakes or scorpions or crocodiles by the hundred were coming over the hills towards you, what would you do?'

'*Heeh*, we would run away in terror,' cried one girl.

'*Kumbe*! Would not the *serikali* - the soldiers and the police, fight them with guns and machines that belch out flames?'

'We fear the jaws of crocodiles, the fangs of snakes and the stings of scorpions, but when the menace that faces us is a small thing to look at we have no fear.'

'What is this menace, Bwana?' shouted a score of voices.

From my pocket I pulled a wide-mouthed bottle. Inside were half a dozen flies. There was a ripple of laughter.

'*Koh, mahazi* - flies! Bwana, they're not a menace. They're everywhere.'

'That's it. And it's because they're everywhere that they're a menace.'

I waved my arms towards a baobab tree. Dramatically Mboga appeared carrying his kerosene tin, his dish, and the gourd of water. He stopped right in front of the girls in the middle of the carefully swept courtyard. He poured the black dust, shaping it like a small volcano and into the crater he poured water.

With a loud buzzing noise Mfupi arrived, wings flapping and spare legs waving. At once Mboga added the dish of greasy slime and Mfupi with active feet stirred up a sizeable and repulsive puddle.

'Bwana, you're making our clean school filthy,' protested a senior girl.

I pretended not to hear and solemnly produced a glass-stoppered brown bottle marked POISON - HIGHLY INFLAMMABLE. A small label underneath read CARBON BI-SULPHIDE. I poured it into the repulsive slush that covered Mfupi's legs and body and wings.

A score of indignant voices burst out. 'Bwana, stop it. That stuff stinks. You're making a disgusting mess outside our kitchen where we keep our clean pots and pans and dishes and baskets. *Yoh*! How that stuff stinks!'

Mfupi was scooping up the horrid concoction and smearing it on his wings. A large girl picked up a broom.

'*Hongo*, Bwana. We come to this school to learn to be clean and tidy and look at this. Look at what you've done.'

I held up my hand. 'Truly. But we have not come merely to make a mess and to turn your clean courtyard into a place of stinking slush. It is because I want to warn you about a disease that is coming and to show you how it spreads. Beware of flies. They are a threat to people's lives and you can be those that make people understand the risk that is threatening us. Flies are dangerous, deadly. They bring all kinds of disease. Flies…'

Mfupi felt I had said enough. It was time for action. In he came buzzing loudly, flapping his mosquito-net wings. He ran from the pool of mud splashing pungent dirt all over the place.

The girls threw up their hands and retreated. 'It's disgusting. Get him out of the place.'

Three of them advanced on the human fly with brooms and Mfupi, who was incredibly messy, started running round the courtyard. The girls were furious. It was the nearest thing to a riot. Mfupi knew exactly what to do. He went to a stack of clean plates daubing them with foulness. He went to the corn baskets and the cooking pots leaving black fingerprints. Then he ran at the girls themselves. They drew back. Some were not quick enough and he laid smelly hands on them and their clothing.

'Bwana, stop him,' they begged. 'It's wrong. It makes us fall sick. Throw him out, Bwana. He's a menace.'

Mfupi's eyes twinkled.

'Have it your way,' I laughed. 'Swat him.'

But, like his insect counterpart, the boy was extremely agile and was well out of the door before a broom could touch him.

'Look at that,' I called to a senior girl as I steered her to look down the microscope.

She peered at the unpleasant sight of a fly's legs. She gasped. '*Yoh*! Horrible. It is…there are not words to describe it.'

'But there are. Listen, everybody. You've seen a picture of this - drama - a play. The foul, filthy mess that young Mfupi made is just the same sort of thing that happens when any fly rests on your food or on you. The difference is that the fly leaves behind something much more deadly than mud and stink. It leaves *dudus* - small germs - that breed incredibly fast and bring sickness, weakness and possibly death.

'If you or your family go to a place where others have this disease of dysentery, realise that flies are your great enemies. They must be swatted, sprayed and killed. They must be kept away from filth and food, otherwise they will surely mix one with the other.'

I pointed to the mud puddle that still remained on the floor. 'In this disease of dysentery, if there is any mess about cover it with sand and bury it or pour boiling water over it before you bury it. Flies must have no chance of getting to it. Do this and we will save many lives. If you take no notice of what you have seen and what you now know scores of people will die. Those at greatest risk are babies and small children.'

Even as I spoke two girls came along with a kerosene tin of boiling water and the whole courtyard was rapidly cleaned up. It was hearteningly obvious by their conversation that these girls were planning action.

9

Trouble in the Wind

In the early afternoon the drum was being beaten with the rhythm that told it was time for medicine to be given. I walked up to the hospital through the field of dry corn stalks. This screened me from the sight of people till I was actually through the gates.

In a place in the women's courtyard where they could see the whole of the track I usually took were four nurses and Maradadi. Today he was wearing a long flowing white garment called a *kanzu* and a bright red fez, obviously brand new. When they saw me the nurses hurried back to the wards.

Maradadi strolled towards me. 'Good afternoon, doctor. I have come to hear the preaching of the hospital.'

Mboga put his head out of the dispensary window and grinned. 'Behold, you don't know the time that we do things here. We tell the words of God in the morning when there are many outpatients.'

Maradadi changed from Swahili into English and said, 'It is inconvenient for me to come in the morning.'

Mboga rolled his eyes and shook his head.

'Maradadi, I plan to talk to the staff about sicknesses for a time then I will give medicines and injections for an hour or so. If you care to wait here I will be glad to talk to you after that.'

'Thank you,' he said. 'And can I make myself useful in the meantime?'

Something did not ring true in his voice but I answered, 'It would help if you would sweep out the outpatients' room and mop the dispensary floor.'

He shrugged his shoulders, rolled up his white *kanzu* and tucked it into his belt. I was intrigued to see that the leg of his purple corduroy trousers was torn at the knee and that he limped when he walked. The events of the night before had left their mark on his person and his clothing but seemed to have done little for his behaviour.

At that moment one of the water carriers stopped beside me. 'Bwana, a hole has arrived in my bucket.'

I had a look. 'Behold, I have medicine for buckets with that sort of trouble. A screw and a nut and washer and the bucket will be itself again. Come over to my office and we'll fix it.'

Thinking that I could not see him, Maradadi put down the broom and hurried past the door. Hefsi came out of the kitchen as I dealt with the bucket. I heard her say the word *chisima* - the well - as I handed the water carrier back his mended bucket.

He said, 'Behold, he who sweeps has finished his job with speed.' He grinned.

Mboga walked up. 'Hodi, Bwana.'

'*Karibu*.' He came in. 'Mboga, would you call the staff together? I want to tell them about the things that happened at the school yesterday. I want to tell them about the trouble that is coming our way - this dysentery.

Soon they had crowded into my office. I stood near the door and related what had happened at the school. Many of them had already heard. They chuckled as I described the dramatic happenings.

'Here at the hospital we must be careful that everything is kept absolutely clean. We must attempt to kill every fly. We will load up a number of *dudu* guns.' I indicated a number of fly sprays we had put out on the table. 'One of the things that Mboga and I are going to do this afternoon is to make a special mixture that kills *dudus* that carry disease by biting and by contaminating food. You know the word contaminate?' They nodded.

'It is flies that we are fighting particularly. They carry dysentery on their legs. We must take the utmost care

with the disgusting side of dysentery. The germs of the disease swarm and swarm. Unless we have special care they will be everywhere.'

At that moment Mfupi arrived at the door with a cardboard box. He had been given clear instructions. He looked at me questioningly. I nodded. Off came the lid of the box and onto the floor cascaded a collection of cockroaches, big black beetles, a couple of scorpions, some small lizards, spiders - all manner of things that creep and crawl and bite.

'*Yoh*!' gasped Hefsi, jumping onto a bench hurriedly. 'I hate those things!'

I nodded. 'And rightly. But think of the *dudus* of dysentery. They're worse than that. They're small but if they get into you they bring great sickness. To be clean is the thing that matters. Follow out the plans that we have made and there will be little danger for any of us. The disease will not spread and the sick people who come in will recover.'

Mfupi was having a busy time gathering up his collection. He was using an old pair of forceps to pick up the scorpions. I was glad when they were all back in the box. I could not expect attention when people were cowering back from hostile insects.

'Perisi,' I said, 'would you be kind enough to go over those points that I have made so that nothing is forgotten.'

She did so with all her teaching skills.

'Thank you,' I said, 'Are your memories now full?' They nodded. 'Now, I have good news. Behold, there on the table you will see tins of pills - medicine with special strength to overcome the disease of dysentery. If people are very sick we give them eight pills when they arrive then, four hours later, four more and then one or two every six hours day and night.'

'*Yoh*,' muttered Hefsi, 'it is heavy work.'

'Heavy work it is, but it means that we can save people's lives and stop much suffering and sadness.'

'We can do it,' said Perisi. Some obviously agreed with her and some just as obviously did not.

Mfupi had put a chameleon on my table. A fly landed not far from it and with incredible swiftness its long tongue flashed out and the fly was no more.

'Why,' asked a junior nurse, 'can *Lwivi* - the chameleon, eat flies that have germs on them and not become ill?'

'There are juices in the stomachs of chameleons which kill germs. They are our friends in this battle.'

I glanced through the window and saw, lounging in the shade, Maradadi listening to all that was going on. He almost collided with Marita who was on duty in the maternity ward.

'Bwana,' she panted. 'A baby has been born and is not breathing. We have done all the usual things with no success.'

'Right, Marita, I'm coming.' I ran and seven minutes later the child let out a sigh and then a lusty yell.

'*Heeh*,' said Marita, sitting down suddenly in her relief.

Sechelela nursed the baby. 'Bwana, that was hectic.'

I wiped the perspiration from my forehead. 'Truly, and it came just at the wrong time. There's trouble brewing in the office. I must get back.'

On the way I heard Yakobo's voice, 'Maradadi, you have nothing to do with the work of the hospital. The Bwana will have no joy in you leaning on the window sill and saying the words that you're saying.'

I came up and tapped Maradadi on the shoulder. 'His words are true. I have no joy in you being here. Unless you have sickness and require medicine, keep away from the hospital. It is clear that you have no desire to help, so *ondoka* - clear out!'

He shrugged his shoulders and strolled slowly towards the gate. Apparently much had been said while I was away.

Hefsi had a jaunty look about her. This was shared by several of her friends who loafed whenever they had the chance, while Perisi and those who were keen on their nursing looked concerned. It was easy to sense that there was trouble in the air.

'Well, everybody, I am trusting you to do your job thoroughly in this emergency. Remember, flies kill more people than lions do. Also, they're much easier to deal with. Now come on, everybody, on with the task.'

For the next hour we were more than busy giving drops for eyes, ointment for ulcers, medicine for coughs, injections for malaria and tick fever. Yakobo came to me as the last patient went out. 'Bwana, there are angry words in many parts of the hospital regarding the dysentery that you say is coming. There are those that will refuse to work. Damage has been done to their wisdom these days.'

'What about you, Yakobo? What are you going to do when we face this trouble?'

'Behold, I thought of the day when Jesus went to the tomb where Lazarus was buried. Did not the relations say to Jesus, "Do not go in there. He's been dead four days. Decay will have started. Do not go." But Jesus went. *Kumbe*! If my Lord will face what is most disagreeable, who am I to shrink back from work that He would do?'

I put out my hand and grasped his. 'Yakobo, you've made me happy. That is exactly what I hoped you would think. This morning as I read the Bible I came across the place where it says what we are both thinking. "A disciple is not above his master but when he is perfectly trained he is like him."'

I heard the sound of someone limping along the path. I thought it might be Maradadi but it turned out to be Elisha.

'Bwana, I am going to look at the well. The water carriers think there is a crack in it. Would you come down with me? I have cement, a couple of trowels, a hammer and a chisel. There is much wisdom in repairing cracks when they are still small. The ladder is ready and the trap door in the roof is open.'

I turned to Yakobo and Elisha. '*Wandugu* - my friends, this is how difficulties need to be tackled: early, before damage has been done. Whether it be cracks in the well or a disease that threatens, there is no doubt that death is lurking in the countryside these days. In the hospital itself I can feel trouble. Would it not be a good idea if here and now we talked to God and told him about the whole matter?'

We knelt together and told God about the entire situation. We asked for wisdom that would help us to do our part and his power to deal with emergencies.

10

Strike and Break-in

We stood on the top of the well.

'*Koh*,' said Elisha. '*Tayari sasa* - ready now. Here are two boxes. We can stand on these and work above water level.'

Working down wells has no joy if you do it in the middle of the day. The tin on the roof makes it so hot that you feel you're in a cooking pot.

'I have brought a lantern so that we can see clearly to work. When we start we must go on till the work is finished.'

I agreed and we climbed down the ladder and prepared to work inside the well. The only indication that anything was happening inside was the open trap door.

We had been quietly at work for half an hour when suddenly a voice came from above. It was hollow and eerie. It startled me and I nearly fell of my box. Elisha pointed to the opening of a water pipe that carried

in the rain water on those rare occasions when we had a thunderstorm. Elisha whispered, 'That pipe is connected to the one which collects the water from the roof of the women's ward.'

The voice said, 'Hefsi, are your there?'

Almost in a whisper came the reply, '*Eheh*, I am here. What's up? Why are you doing this? I must be careful. Sechelela is at the end of the verandah.'

Maradadi's voice replied, 'Have no fear. No one can hear us. This is a useful way of speaking to you. These are my instructions. Make all the girls discontented. Talk many words of grumbling and arrange that there is an angry *shauri* with the Bwana. Let there be loud words and shouting and threats.'

I looked across at Elisha and put my finger to my lips. I wondered what was behind this piece of trickery.

Hefsi started to speak but the words faded into a gasp. Then she spoke again with urgency, 'No more now. I must go. Mwendwa is coming towards our ward.'

Silence once again came into the well.

'*Heeh*,' breathed Elisha, 'this is a bad thing. I have sorrow in my heart for that girl Hefsi. For many days she has tried to do the right thing. She has heard the words of God and tried to follow them but then came temptation. She listened to it and…' he shook his head. '*Yoh*, Bwana, you do not know the evil ways of her relations. Truly, they follow the path of *shaitan* - the devil. She is like the trees upon the hill, Bwana. The wind has blown on them when they were small and they all slant in the direction that the east wind blows. Do not be angry with her. Do what you can to help her even though it was because of her that Daudi chose to go the wrong path.'

We settled back to the job of cementing up a crack in the side of the well which we had carefully probed and packed. It was shortly after sundown when we emerged from the top of the well.

Standing outside the office was Hefsi. 'Bwana, there are those of us who would have words with you.'

'And what would those words be about?'

'Bwana, we have words of complaint. Many of us in the hospital have no joy. Behold…'

At that moment Sechelela arrived - a very irate Sechelela. 'Bwana, it is now the hour of sundown. There are those who come on duty at this hour and they have not appeared. Mwendwa is the only one working.'

'*Koh*!' snapped Hefsi. 'The words of the nurses are that they are tired.'

'Where are they?'

'Just walking, Bwana, walking round having a look at the country.'

'*Hongo*, are they now? And what about the sick ones?'

The girl tilted her chin and said, '*Tumekwisha kufanya striki* - we have gone on strike.'

'This is a serious matter, Hefsi. We certainly must talk it through at once. Call the other nurses and bring them into the lecture room. I will meet you there in twenty minutes.'

While the nurses were being brought back from their walkabout I went to talk to the sister who was slowly recovering from severe malaria. 'Bibi, we are in trouble up at the hospital. Added to all the other things they've hit on another idea now - a strike. They didn't think of it themselves but a character who pushes drugs has come to the village. He has stirred things up. Do you think you feel fit enough to come and help me with this *shauri* - discussion?'

She nodded. 'I'll come straight away.'

A few minutes later in the lecture room we turned to the nurses. 'You want to have words with us?'

Silence.

'What is the trouble?'

Silence.

'Why have you decided to go off duty? Have your tongues lost their strength?'

A couple of them giggled.

'Well, if you have no words the thing to do is to go back on duty in the wards.'

Here Hefsi broke in angrily, 'We refuse.'

'But why?'

'Sister,' said another of the nurses, 'we read about a strike in the *Gazetti*. We thought it a good idea especially when the work is not pleasant.'

The sister looked at her and smiled. 'Was that the only reason?'

'*Hongo*!' interrupted Hefsi, 'We don't like the food, Bibi.'

'Did you tell anyone about it?'

There was a tense silence. 'Would you get food as good as this at home?'

Again silence.

There was no hint of anger in the voice of this splendid woman who had given the cream of her life for these girls and others like them. 'Come,' she said, 'you're not following the ways of wisdom. Something has come into your minds which has upset you. You've been listening to words which have no profit in them.'

'*Koh*,' retorted Hefsi, 'we want a change. Also, Bibi, we have no joy in the thought of this disease that the Bwana says is coming - this dysentery.'

'Hefsi, did I have any words of refusal in the days when you had that great ulcer on your leg - days when you had much pain, when your ulcer was not food for anybody's nose? Did I refuse to help you when that work was disagreeable?'

Hefsi looked at the ground. The sister went on, 'You are Christians, are you not?' Most of the nurses nodded their heads. 'Well, if you are, when you come against anything in your life that's like this, it is wisdom to talk to Jesus about it. Have you asked him what he thought about your strike and your refusals?'

The silence could be felt. She knelt down beside the chair. 'I'm going to ask him about it now. Will you join me?' Some of the girls knelt. Others of them sat looking stubborn.

I felt a light tap on my shoulder. Elisha beckoned to me urgently. 'Bwana, while you have been talking in there, Maradadi took the opportunity to break open your medicine cupboard with a large screw driver. The old man who was blind till you operated on him a week ago saw it all happen. He did not realise that anything wrong was happening but Maradadi has gone and a tin of the dysentery pills with him.'

'*Hongo*, Elisha, that's bad. Now I see what he was up to. He wanted to get the staff out of the way while he did his own bit of burglary. This is bad. There is only one good thing about it. He has five hundred of those pills but three and a half thousand are in my house and safe.'

'But, doctor, five hundred of these pills could do so much.'

'They might well mean that twenty or thirty lives could be saved. Maradadi is an evil man. This matters nothing to him.'

The carpenter nodded. 'I was reading today in the Bible and it said, "Make no mistake. You can't laugh at God. Whatever you sow, that you reap."'

'Elisha, the evil seed that Maradadi is sowing can produce a vicious harvest for himself.'

Hefsi stood in the office doorway. In a loud

angry voice she shouted, 'I am leaving the hospital. *Koh*, why should I work here any longer!'

'*Hongo*,' said Elisha quietly, 'she, too, is inviting trouble.'

11
Whirlwind

Mboga rushed round the corner. 'Quickly, Bwana, a great wind storm is close. But there is still time to put up all the shutters.'

The last of these was in place when it started. First it was dust and then came the grit. It felt as though we were in the middle of the Sahara desert.

Elisha was perched on the roof nailing down a piece of corrugated iron. He climbed down hurriedly, putting the ladder on the ground and pointed with his chin to the red cloud overhead. 'See, Bwana, there goes the good earth from the place where they are planting. Does not *ivunde* - the wind, show his wrath by sweeping away much of the countryside?'

On the road to the hospital, some distance away, we could see people running in terror and then throwing themselves flat on the ground.

Mboga was shading his eyes. 'Bwana, behold, I have never seen one as large as that before.'

We gazed at the huge twisted pillar of red dust.

There was a dull roar as it swept up the hill. Deliberately it seemed to turn and make its way towards us. Shrill screams of alarm came from people in and round the hospital.

Mboga shouted, 'Down on the ground, Bwana, flat! It's coming to attack us.'

Lying on the ground I could see swirling gusts of raging wind over an area the size of a football field. It sucked up grass and sticks and hurled them high into the air, then the huge writhing pillar in the centre came shrieking down on us. It hurled a woman with a baby on her back cruelly to the ground. A man holding a small boy by the hand was some way behind her. I saw them stagger. Then we were in strange red darkness. With a screech of torn metal the outpatients' verandah was split apart. The mud-and-wattle hospital kitchen was swept away and again came the ear-torturing sound of iron being ripped off rafters. For a moment we caught an awesome glimpse of sheets of corrugated iron soaring skywards as though they were leaves.

'Down, Bwana!' Elisha shouted huskily. 'There's more. 'It'll…' His voice was lost.

Again came the red darkness and I realised that we had for a long moment been in the eye of the whirlwind and then, as suddenly as it had started, it was gone. Sand and grit and fine dust rained down on us and through it all the setting sun looked like an enormous red ball.

I was aware of Elisha sitting on the ground rubbing a spot that was rapidly swelling on his forehead. This didn't worry him. He was looking at the lacerated wall

and the twisted iron of some of the nearby buildings and at the rafters snapped off jaggedly. In the distance came the crash of sheet iron landing amongst the baobab trees.

'*Heeh*! said the carpenter, 'there is much work for me to do here.'

The brute force of *ifulafumbi* had hacked out its crooked path. Strangely, the ground ten metres on either side was free from damage. Then I remembered the woman I had seen hurled to the ground. She was lying amongst the cornstalks unconscious with the baby still on her back. There was a nasty gash over her eye. Her husband was vainly trying to recover the blanket which a little while before had been round his shoulders but was now on the top of a sizeable thorn tree.

'I shall bring a stretcher,' said Mboga and set off at a run.

Perisi and Sechelela were quickly on the scene. They swung the baby from the woman's back. A moment later he let out a lusty yell. 'He will recover, Bwana,' smiled Sechelela.

But the mother lay still and her pulse was very weak. She was quickly carried to the ward. Clutching his father's hand and whimpering behind us came the small boy. The man was stuttering out incoherent sentences putting the blame for the whirlwind to the account of some of his hostile ancestors.

'What about the woman?' said Sechelela.

'A dressing for that cut, and keep her warm and let her rest till she becomes conscious again, then call me.'

Sechelela whispered, 'Bwana, are you remembering that Elisha was hit on the head by a stone? He has a swelling that must be bringing him no joy whatsoever.'

I patted her on the shoulder and smiled. 'Oh, my grandmother, you're a woman of worth and indeed you are a splint to my memory.'

Her hair was completely white. She chuckled and her eyes twinkled. In Swahili she said, '*Fanya kazi*! Get on with the job!'

Elisha was sitting on a stool outside the door. He and I both had odd pink complexions from the dust. Hurrying towards us was a clean and spruce looking Mfupi carrying a tray with a dish of warm water, swabs, and three tubes of ointment.

'That is good, Mfupi. Thank you for helping.'

The boy stood and watched as I bathed Elisha's forehead and gently rubbed ointment into the swelling that was the size of a hen's egg. 'This medicine takes the swelling out of bruises.'

'*Eheh*, Bwana, medicine of strength. Already the pain becomes less.'

I bandaged Elisha's forehead. He fingered the place. 'That is good, Bwana.' He carefully put on his fez and said, 'When you were talking about Maradadi and the dysentery pills that he stole you said "whatever we sowed we would reap". I know that if you plant millet you get millet and if you plant melon seeds you grow melons. This morning as I read the Bible I saw that there were those who had no time for God. They refused to obey His orders and they chose to worship silver and gold instead of Almighty God and I read, "They sow the wind and they shall reap the whirlwind". Many times have I seen *ifulafumbi* stagger across the countryside doing damage as he went, but never have I understood the matter as I do today. But, Bwana, after what we have seen this afternoon who would care to have a harvest of whirlwinds?'

'The trouble is, Elisha, when people sow sin in their lives they don't even think of the harvest. Take Maradadi who has stolen pills from us which could mean so much in the disease that makes people's stomachs jump.'

As I spoke the woman who had been knocked unconscious by the whirlwind sat up. Huskily she said, 'Bwana, where is my child? It is for the reason that his stomach jumps that I've brought him to the hospital. He is a sick one.' She tried unsuccessfully to stagger to her feet.

In the excitement of that late afternoon I had forgotten all about the small boy. He lay huddled up at the bottom of the steps. It was obvious what his trouble was. Our dysentery epidemic had begun.

12
Epidemic

Perisi bent over the small sick boy. '*Koh*, he is burning hot.'

'He is indeed. Notice, too, that his skin is wrinkled like that of old people. He has lost much water from his body because of this disease. We call this dehydration.

'Now, first the medicines and the fluids. We must coax him to drink. If he is too weak for that we must spoon it in. If he can't swallow we must use a tube. As for medicine, it's all a matter of the size of the sick one. For children, start with four tablets then two in six hours.'

The sulpha pills powdered up beautifully. I mixed the powder with sweetened water and watched the nurse spoon it down his throat.

I walked to the window. The shutters had been folded back. Red dust filled every crack and crevice. It was very dark. I blinked. In the middle of the place where we grew corn was a weird patch of pale, quavery light. Up through it rocketed a shovel and a triumphant, though muffled, voice shouted, '*Basi!* That's the end of it!'

Elisha came out of the shadows. 'Wait!' he shouted. 'Let me check the work.'

He climbed down the ladder which was beneath the surface. There was some confused mumbling and then laughter. Elisha appeared above the surface followed by the two muscular men who had been doing the digging.

Elisha called across to me. 'Bwana, all is ready. The great hole is at the right depth. At dawn tomorrow I will come and put up the cornstalk screen.'

In the dim light of the lantern I saw Mfupi picking up the shovel. He came to the door of the ward. 'Bwana, the small boy has made a mess outside the ward. I shall clear it up now that the hole is to be used.'

Elisha came behind him. 'This is an important thing, Bwana, for as everybody knows flies do not come in darkness but with first light they will be here.'

'And was that not the reason why the hole was dug so deep?'

Perisi reported quietly, 'The medicine is inside the child and there is no problem with fluids. He can swallow.'

'That's splendid. You will notice that he lies on a rubber sheet and on that is newspaper because...'

She hurried across to the small boy's bed. 'I see the reason.' She shook her head. 'Oh, yes, I see the reason.'

'Fold it up with care, Perisi, and down the hole it goes. Then wash your hands thoroughly. There will be much washing of the hands these days.'

Mfupi was at the door with his outstretched shovel. 'Put the paper in this, Perisi. I have cleaned up everything outside.'

'Well done. And now for rest. We will need all our strength for the time that is ahead. Should we put a lantern near this hole? It would be an unhappy thing for anybody who fell into it in the night.'

Mfupi shook his head. 'No hospital person walks through the old corn garden at night. Only hyenas.'

He chuckled. 'Wouldn't it be nice for a hyaena to fall in tonight?'

The sun was just showing up over the far hills.

'*Hodi*,' called a voice. '*Hodi, hodi.*'

I woke. It was Elisha. He was usually a sombre person. He would smile and occasionally chuckle but here outside my window he was holding his sides with laughter. Tears were running down his face.

'What's up, *fundi*?'

There was so much laughter bubbling out of him that it took a time to tell his story.

'I went to put up the screen round our new hole and there was a voice coming from deep down. It was full of fear. I knew that voice. So did Mboga. There was little light in the corn garden and anyone not knowing of yesterday's diggings, anyone who chose not to follow the path...' There was another explosion of laughter. 'As you know Mboga has skill in imitating.

You should hear him use your voice and making the mistakes you make in speaking Chigogo.'

By this time I was half dressed. 'Come on,' I urged, 'tell me what happened.'

'The man down the hole is terrified. Mboga is making hyaena sounds. He says he wants you to come because you need laughter, which is hard to find in a dysentery epidemic.'

By this time I was ready. We hurried up the path together. As we neared the gate I heard the cry of a hungry hyaena, a most scary sound. Mboga stood some twenty paces from the hole. In the early morning light I could see his finger on his lips. He stretched out his neck, his chin pointing towards the brilliant colouring of the sunrise and produced hair-raising hyaena laughter.

From below ground came a gasp. '*Yayagwe*!'

Elisha clamped his hand over his mouth and gulped. 'He calls his mother.'

A piece of newspaper was being filled with mud. Then came Mboga's angry shout. 'Clear out, you foul beast. Do you want to suffer from this dysentery disease? Keep away from that hole. Get out of our hospital.'

There was the sound of stones being thrown and the yelp of a hyaena on the run. Then came Mboga's usual voice. 'Yes, that's the place to throw it.'

Sechelela and the two boys, Mfupi and Pungu, had come into view and were watching open-mouthed.

On droned the voice, 'We only started using it yesterday. Yes, give it to me. I'll throw it in and that bucket too.' In went the newspaper pack. In went the dish of water.

From the hole came an agonised yell. 'Help me. Don't throw in filth. I'm down here. I didn't know. I fell in.'

'Who are you?' demanded Mboga, trying to keep the grin out of his voice.

'It is I, Maradadi.'

'But what are you doing in the hospital grounds at night? And the Bwana ordered you not to come in here unless you had sickness and required medicine.'

'I was just walking around.'

'But that's forbidden.'

Pathetic tones came from the bottom of the hole. 'Help me. Get me out. Please. I'll give you money.'

'I'll go and ask the Bwana.'

The voice was shrill now. 'Don't! Don't call the Bwana.'

Quietly Mboga walked over to me. 'Bwana, I shall put the ladder down and get him out. He will be no more bother to us. I shall get him out and scare him properly.'

'Is there any chance of getting back any of the pills he stole?'

'He's too cunning to have them here, Bwana. They will be well hidden and his mouth will be full of lies.'

I went into the ward. The small boy had made dramatic progress. His mother was delighted. 'See his skin, Bwana. It is again that of a child. His stomach still jumps but much less.'

I smiled down at her. 'The medicine is good. He now has the proper amount of water inside him. He lost much fluid in the early hours of this sickness.' She nodded happily.

I looked through the window. Mboga was shaking his fist at a retreating figure. I could not hear his exact words but there were angry threats in them.

Elisha had four kerosene tins: two full of water, two empty. The full ones were over a small fire and would soon be boiling.

Sechelela talked to the staff. There was a table outside the door.

'If you touch the sick people with this disease or any of the mess they produce, wash your hands. Take a gourd full. Put it in the basin. Use soap and then pour the water into the empty kerosene tin.'

'Remember,' shouted Elisha, 'we have little water these days and it has to be carried half an hour's journey from the wells.'

Sechelela nodded. 'He speaks truth. When the tin is three-quarters full it will be put on the fire again. The *vidudu* - the germs, cannot live if they are boiled. And see, there is another tin here. Into this goes everything that will be thrown down the hole.'

'I shall find a lid for it,' said Mfupi. 'There must be no opportunity for the flies.'

'All this is wisdom. Follow it with care,' I urged.

Yakobo was hurrying towards me. 'Bwana, there is a messenger from the chief at Ilolo. He brings a letter.'

Printed in pencil was a letter which read:

To the doctor. Greetings. I am well and those of my village are well but there are many who are suffering from stomachs that jump. Their strength is gone. Their skin is stretched tight on their bones. There are seventeen people here and we do not have enough men in the village to carry them in. Will you come that they may be taken to the hospital in your truck?

The request left no doubt that the epidemic had arrived but our ancient vehicle was highly unreliable and a horror to drive.

I called this one and that. Beds were to be made ready and everything prepared for immediate treatment of those whose lives would be in danger. Mattresses were hastily put into the back of the truck.

They were covered with rubber sheets and a large mosquito net draped to keep the flies out. The radiator was filled with water and the tyres pumped up to the right pressure for there were wide stretches of sand in which we could easily bog on that safari.

I made a final survey of the hospital. Pungu came with me armed with his *bomba* - the insecticide spray. He set to work vigorously spraying the wire gauze of the windows. His white teeth showed in a broad smile. 'Bwana, that's the bed I was in.' He pointed with his chin to the one in the corner.

'*Eheh*, I remember. Did not many people say that you had reached the end of your safari on earth?'

He nodded emphatically. 'I remember well, Bwana.'

'And do you remember the injections, Pungu?'

'*Yoh!*' He rubbed himself tenderly in the least patched portion of his shorts. '*Yoh*, Bwana. Will I ever forget? And how busy the ward was then. But behold, now six empty beds.'

'True, but in two hours' time that won't be so.'

On the back of an envelope I jotted the figure 6. To find seventeen beds suddenly in a small jungle hospital is nothing short of a conjuring trick. In the women's ward were three beds neatly made, covered with patch-work quilts. The ward was colourful with its white-washed walls and scrubbed grey concrete floor.

In the sterilising room of the operating theatre I could hear the roar of a primus. Yakobo was carefully supervising an apparatus for distilling water while ten wide-mouthed bottles were cooking merrily in half a kerosene tin of boiling water.

'Bwana,' he reassured me, 'in an hour's time we will have ten bottles filled with sterilised glucose and saline solution. The needles and the rubber tubing will all be ready when you return.'

'We're going to need them, Yakobo. We must be prepared to work day and night.'

Then I went and checked the sanitary arrangements of the hospital. These were in charge of a fierce looking old man who rejoiced in the name of *Ihowe* - the crow.

He was so called because of the wily glitter in his eye. The efficient running of his part of the battle against disease was vitally important. I explained about the new deep hole and its use.

Then came the toot of the horn. I walked to the gate calling, 'Don't forget, Ihowe, you've got the biggest job in the hospital now,' and I saw the old man nod his head.

Elisha was repairing the whirlwind damage. I went across. 'I know you're a carpenter but if old Ihowe is not doing his job properly remind him with your hammer.'

Elisha tilted back his red fez and chuckled.

13
Hospital! Urgent!

Mboga and the chief's messenger were waiting for me as I climbed behind the wheel. It was only six kilometres to Ilolo but there was not even the hint of a road. For good measure there were five rivers to cross, all of them a hundred metres wide and filled with the soft sand that made driving a nightmare. We battled across the second one with considerable difficulty.

'*Yoh!*' said the chief's messenger. 'Behold, it is a road for feet not for wheels.'

'You speak truly but there are ways to improve it. Here are two spades. Get the people to cut the salt bush that grows beside the river and put it in the wheel-marks of the truck and then cover it with earth. Do it well so that we may travel back with speed. People will die if we're bogged in that sand.'

He nodded. 'Truly.'

I coaxed the truck up the rough track and thankfully climbed the last hill.

The village was in turmoil. Outside one long mud-and-wattle house were a group of people groaning with misery. The chief greeted me and together we went from house to house. I gave some injections and doses of medicine and urged that all drinking water should be boiled. The whole place stank. The filth, the squalor, the flies, were overpowering.

'What can we do?' muttered the chief.

'Many must be taken to hospital. This is a disease that threatens life. And there is much for you to do here.'

We talked about the first principles of hygiene. He nodded. 'Can you send someone who knows about this to guide us?'

'I will try, Great One, but with all these sick people the hospital will need every pair of hands available.'

'But, Bwana, if we can stop people becoming sick in the villages then you will have less work to do in the hospital.'

I shook him by the hand. 'Chief, you have spoken words of wisdom. Let them not be forgotten in the days that are ahead.'

Soon we had ten women and children packed liked sardines in the back of the truck. The mosquito net, now tucked in carefully, was literally black with flies.

Pungu was spraying them and describing to all who would listen how dangerous flies were.

'Are you coming back, Bwana?'

'Yes, Pungu, but it will be some time. These people must be treated.'

'Shall I stay here and spray the place and tell them about the hole and the things that Mfupi is doing?'

I looked questioningly at the chief.

'Does the boy know these things?' he asked.

'He has wisdom in these matters.'

'Well, let him stay.'

I took Pungu aside. 'Don't forget about washing hands. Get them to dig a hole even if it isn't very deep. Put the mess into it and cover it up.'

'All this I will do, Bwana. My eyes have been opened these days and when I was ill I saw many things which I have not forgotten.'

A woman rushed up to me. 'Bwana, Bwana, have pity. Take my child also. Will he not die if you leave him here? Take him that he may have medicine quickly.'

I leaned over the wheel. 'Be at peace. I will return. Your child shall have medicine.'

As we drove away I prayed. The task ahead would be a severe test of the hospital, of its equipment and the endurance of our few remaining staff.

Mboga leant towards me. 'Bwana, are you praying?'

'I am, Mboga, but my eyes are open. You don't need to have them shut or to be kneeling to talk to God and we so need his help at the moment.'

I swung the truck into the first of the five riverbeds thankful for a row of bushes packed into the tyre tracks. These gave the wheels a chance to bite into the sand.

'That's better,' said Mboga. 'And it will be even better later for they will put in earth and stones.'

'It will need to be,' I shouted as we skidded wildly.

Mboga leapt out and pushed. I swung the wheel and we crabbed our way out sideways. We all sighed with relief as Sukuma struggled up the far side safely.

Panting, Mboga jumped in beside me. '*Yoh*, Bwana, as I pushed I remembered the words that I read the other morning, "I can do all things through Christ who strengthens me." Truly, Bwana, I shall be praying much these days.'

Thoughts of Mboga's words helped as we drove perilously across dry riverbed after dry riverbed. We did not speak again until we climbed the last bank.

'*Yoh*, Spinach, that's the fifth. You were right about being able to do all things through God's strength. We're doing his work for his purpose. He knows our difficulties.'

We pulled up outside the gate and in next to no time the hospital was alive with action. Elisha climbed down from the roof. '*Yoh*, Bwana, it looks like an ants' nest that has been stirred up.'

We watched sick people going to the various wards. Some could walk but those who couldn't were carried on stretchers.

'There is hot water available,' said the carpenter. 'I cut an oil drum in half.'

The staff were thankful. There was bathing of patients and taking of temperatures. I worked fast, examining and prescribing. The whole situation was far from straightforward. Many of the sick ones had malaria as well as being seriously ill with dysentery. The chaotic symptoms of this disease played havoc with the normal routine. I had only two more patients to see when a nurse came hurrying into the room.

'Bwana, the child called Nhonya is vomiting. Behold the pills she has taken are lost. They will not stay inside her.' There were ways of getting round this problem and I took them.

Ahead was another journey over those five daunting dry riverbeds. It was vital to bring in another truck-load of sick people. Their lives depended on them being in hospital. It would have made a considerable difference if Daudi had been with us. But Daudi was at the peanut planting.

Elisha walked past the window. '*Habari*?' he asked.

'The news is good, but it would be much better if you would come with me to the village of Ilolo and explain to them how they can best fight the dysentery infection in the village.'

Elisha scratched his head. 'I am a carpenter, Bwana.'

'True, and a good one.'

It was only the afternoon but fatigue seemed to close in around me like a thick fog. I carefully washed my hands and splashed water over my face, sat for a minute then went to the last patient, a small boy who lay in a cot. He looked as though he was asleep but as I felt his pitifully thin stomach he opened his eyes.

'*Yoh*, Bwana, your hands are warm. And all my body is cold; my inside is cold and my tongue is dry.'

I smiled at him. 'Have you thirst?'

'*Eheh*, Bwana, I have thirst.'

'Chew up the pills I will give you and drink the medicine and then keep drinking water, sip by sip, even as a chicken drinks. Do this and before long strength will come back and warmth within you.'

I walked out of the ward. The key members of the staff were waiting. 'Bwana!' Yakobo shook his head. 'It's too big for us. We can't deal with all of this. I don't know what to do.'

'Do you feel as though a thick cloud has come over you?'

They all nodded. 'It is that, Bwana.'

Old Sechelela had a forlorn look over her usually tranquil face. 'And I am old, Bwana.'

'I am not,' said Perisi, 'but I'm tired, so tired.'

Pepetua nodded. 'I have fears that I will make mistakes. I seem to walk in a dream.'

'Come, let us sit in the office and we will talk to God.'

Mboga looked at me and raised his eyebrows. I nodded. 'The key to the store, Bwana. These are times when there is much need for sugar.' My smile was a weary one. We sat down and one after the other prayed to God for the strength to do what seemed impossible. I could hear a shuffling of feet and a tinkling of tea cups. We finished praying. There was Mboga pouring tea and ladling in spoonfuls of sugar.

Sechelela was sitting back in her chair sound asleep.

'How badly we need at least two more trained people. And what a difference it would make if the reluctant ones would become willingly busy.'

'Do you think God will answer?' asked Perisi.

'I do.'

'Do you feel that he is doing it?'

'Feelings aren't worth much, Perisi, especially when tiredness sits on your chest. It's faith that counts.'

'And what about your faith?' asked Sechelela, who was now wide awake and stirring her tea.

'I'm afraid the legs of my faith are not strong, but it's not me that matters. It's God. Remember his words, "Even though I walk through the valley of the shadow of death I will fear no evil for you are with me, your rod and your staff they comfort me."'

14
Second-hand Water

Mboga walked across to the corner of the room and picked up a stick with a knob on the end - a powerful weapon. Then he made aggressive noises.

He grinned, 'Once I hit a hyaena with one of these. He was after my goat. *Yoh*, I thumped him. He howled and ran but not fast. His ribs would never be the same.'

'What are you telling me, Mboga?'

'His rod and his staff, they comfort, they protect. It's his arm that does it.' He chuckled. 'The little goat could do nothing by itself.'

Sechelela was looking through the window. 'Three people come to the hospital.'

'Sick ones?' Tiredness made my voice husky.

'*Yoh*,' exclaimed Pepetua, 'is it not Bibi, and with her, Sala, who is a trained nurse? And that is her husband, Yona, the one who sings.'

I hurried out of the door and gripped the Australian nurse by the hand. 'Bibi, you're not fit for work yet.'

'I can manage,' she smiled. 'I'll do the mothers-and-babies end of things with Marita and Seche, and Sala will help in the ward. She used to be in charge there.'

I broke in, 'And Yona will help me pick up more sick people?' Yona nodded.

Perisi and Mboga in one breath said, 'Rod and staff.'

I was on my feet. 'Yona, will you come with me to Ilolo? Elisha also. Mboga, you go to sleep and I'll wake you up when we bring the next load of patients.'

Pepetua made a wry face. 'It's the same old story, Sala. We will have to put sick ones on the floor in my ward, but we'll have everything ready.'

I sighed. 'That's what happens in epidemics. Pep, you show Sala how we are treating the folk and the routine we have set up to protect the staff, then you too go and have some rest.'

'Bwana,' announced Elisha, 'we have washed out the back of the truck. Water is scarce so we used the spray pump.'

'A way of wisdom. Now come on, we must make our safari.'

Yona stood looking at the truck. 'This grandmother of machines has difficulty with the road, Bwana?'

'We got there this morning but only just.' We climbed aboard and started the motor by pushing her down the hill.

The carpenter said anxiously, 'Behold, she limps like I do.'

Yona shook his head. 'She is sick, Bwana.'

We crossed the first river without much difficulty and the second. Yona looked at the steep banks of the third. 'Stop, Bwana. She will refuse and we will be stuck. It is the sickness of spark plugs and points.'

'He's a *fundi*,' explained Elisha. 'Did he not work for George, the Greek, in his garage at Dodoma?'

'It won't take long,' Yona assured me. 'Rest, Bwana, while I work.'

I stretched out on the driver's seat. It was bliss to shut my eyes. Vaguely I was aware of mechanical noises and then a deep voice singing tunefully. In my dreamy state I translated the words back into my mother tongue:

I will not stop singing.
My song shall bear witness
That on the cross Jesus died for my sins.
 Jesus told me
Watch and pray
Eyes open wide.

Jesus is coming again.

He will find his sign on my forehead.

So I won't stop singing

On the cross he died that I might be forgiven.

Then with considerable skill he whistled the tune and I was asleep. But not for long.

The engine started and I found myself propped up between my two African friends. With a roar and a bump we were across the bad river. I was only fully awake when we came out of the fifth and could see the village ahead of us.

'Elisha, you will check up on all the hygiene arrangements?'

He nodded. 'And I shall walk home. There is a moon tonight.'

I saw that he was gripping a knobbed stick. He looked at it and grinned.

Yona was obviously a capable driver. Much of my time could be saved if he took over the collecting of those who were dangerously ill.

Beyond the village a mirage shimmered over the plains and in the distance a whirlwind swirled its drunken way over the countryside. There were dozens of villages between us and the blue row of hills in the distance. My heart sank as I thought of what might be happening in them.

Again it seemed only a matter of minutes before the truck was full of sick people. As Yona fitted up the tail-board I looked at the mass of sick folk crowded together in that small space. The whole picture might easily have been a page from a famine report. The people looked starved and hopeless, their eyes deep sunken. They seemed to have barely enough interest in life to open them. Their arms and legs hung limply and their skin looked like old parchment. These same people three days before had been cheerful and healthy, doing the everyday things of African life.

Our hospital, limited as it was, was the only spot where some quarter of a million people could hope for medicine that worked and facilities to put them back on their feet.

I felt a touch on my arm. It was Pungu. 'Bwana, the people have listened to me. Many of them are following the ways of wisdom.'

'Good man. Thank you for doing all you have. Elisha will carry on. You come back to the hospital and eat and rest.'

As Yona drove back to the hospital I suddenly realised how we could help even the sickest of our patients to understand about God. Music finds its way into the minds even of those barely conscious and plants itself in the memory.

Yona seemed to sense what I was thinking. Softly he started to sing:

So I'll not stop my song,
The words of which carry life along.
On the cross he died
That I might be forgiven.

The boy sitting beside me, sagging with tiredness,

suddenly sat up. 'That is the medicine, Bwana Yona. Play on your *ilimba* and sing the words of God to the sick people.'

Yona changed gear, climbed the steep river bank and looked across at me. With a smile I nodded. 'He's right. That's the medicine.'

We swung in through the hospital gate and again the truck was unloaded. The sick lay on the verandah.

A cheerful stocky little man, Jason the mason, a close friend of Elisha, ran across to me. 'Bwana, before you do anything else, come and see my work.' I followed him into the bathroom, a small room with an ankle-high concrete ridge dividing it into two.

'Water is our great need and we are short of it so I have cleaned the drainpipe thoroughly.'

He pointed to the hole in the smooth concrete floor and, picking up a battered stirrup pump, he nudged a heavy iron square tin. 'The tin holds enough but not too much, and *bomba*, the pump, is fixed so that it will only produce a fine spray and no water will be wasted. The sick one is placed in there and can easily be washed.'

Then his eyes lit up. 'But the special cunning of the matter is this. The water runs down the pipe and into a large oil drum.' He stopped for breath.

'But, wordy one, it's dirty water.'

'True, Bwana, but not too dirty to wash the floor and the rubber sheets. Also, I have other ways of wisdom to save water. The hand washing basin is now on the verandah with two kerosene tins, one full, one empty. There is also a jam tin beside the full one. I have made a wire handle for it. Those that wash fill this small tin, pour it into the basin, wash their hands and then empty the water they have used into the empty kerosene tin. Not a drop is wasted. This water can be used to wash floors and, if we are very short, to wash people.'

I enjoyed a laugh. 'This is good wisdom, Jason, for water plays a most important part in this illness. Sick people lose so much water. They need to drink frequently or they die. Look at those on the verandah now.'

He shook his head. 'Their skin looks like a goat hide that has been left out in the sun. Truly, it is the work of one person to help the children to drink enough and also to assist the people who have not strength to lift up their hands.'

'You speak truly, Jason. This ward, packed tight with people, needs someone giving drinks all the time, but, as you can see, it is not pleasant work.'

He wrinkled his nose. The place stank. Pepetua was collecting fouled sheets of newspaper and wiping down the rubber sheeting. She smiled across at me. 'Wouldn't it be nice if we had gloves?'

I nodded, but 'Scrub your hands, Pep,' was all I could say.

Outside the door I saw Mfupi taking all this rubbish away to the deep hole. Jason stood beside me. 'Bwana, Elisha is a carpenter and he is telling people how to fight this disease in the villages. I will help by looking after the water supply and giving water to sick children. Have I not a family? Do I not understand about children? See, already I am prepared for the work.' He pointed to our largest teapot. 'It's full of water that has been boiled and is now cold.' He spoke at high speed. 'I shall return soon. I will fix the men's ward bathroom in the same way as this one if you agree.'

I put my hands on his muscular shoulders. 'Thank you, Jason. Do so. I will give you a new name. You are now Bwana Malenga, the water boss.'

I heard his pleased laugh as he hurried away. The squeak of the stirrup pump sounded and I saw patient after patient, newly washed, being brought into the ward, some led, some carried.

15
Night Duty

The ward was packed with patients. The beds had been removed and mattresses covered the floor. We moved the ward table out onto the verandah and then, being careful not to tread on people, I moved from one to the other examining and ordering medicine.

Yakobo came behind me taking blood samples. He whispered, 'I'm sorry, but it will be late tomorrow before we have all these ready.'

'Truly, I understand, but I will give injections to anyone I suspect may have malaria.'

The sun was beginning to set. Hurricane lamps were lighted. I picked up the clipboard. Everyone was listed on it and their treatment was noted. Three of the teachers from the girls' school came and greeted me, 'Doctor, is there anything we can do to help?'

'There is indeed. Could you cut up this sheet of cardboard and put string through the pieces? I want to put labels round everyone's neck and write on those labels when they have their treatment and what it has been. We cannot afford to miss anybody.'

'We'll do it, Bwana.'

They worked briskly and in half an hour each patient wore a label and pills were given out.

'I cannot swallow. It will choke me,' gasped one sick woman.

'Chew the pills first, then drink.' She did so. I wrote on her card.

'Bwana,' she croaked, 'is that a charm that is round my neck?'

'No, not a charm,' I told her, 'but it is very important.'

All who could swallow did so. Then came the difficult business of treating those who could not swallow or who would not swallow.

I turned to Pepetua. 'Pep, we'll do the "cannots" first. They will give no trouble.'

We slipped slim rubber tubes down their throats and fixed a small funnel at the top end. Before pouring anything in we listened. If we heard sounds of breathing we pulled it back several inches and tried again. When there was no noise we knew the tube was in the stomach and began to pour in medicine and water. This took time.

When we came to those who clenched their teeth and struggled it was more difficult. Jason bent down. 'Bwana, leave these to me. I'll see they do it.'

It was a relief to me to see how successful he was. Utterly tired, I went through the hand washing routine and walked wearily to my house, showered with three

litres of water, drank two cups of tea and had a snack. Then I settled back in an armchair that Elisha had made from packing cases, and slept.

I was forced back into wakefulness by the battered alarm clock. It was half past eleven at night. I splashed water into my face and walked up to the men's ward. Sitting on a stool in front of the door was Pastor Daniel. I greeted him. 'Pastor, are you sick?'

He smiled cheerfully. 'No, I am working here. Your helpers have tiredness so I said that I would come and make sure that all of the sick men have water to drink and that they drink it. They said that you would come and give the pills.'

I gripped his hand. 'Bwana Daniel, you have greatly encouraged me. Let us take the opportunity of praying together for the many people whose lives could so easily be lost. Here we can save them.'

Pill swallowing went smoothly till we came to a ten-year-old. I could barely feel his pulse. The pastor was amazed when I manipulated the thin tube into the boy's stomach and poured in powdered pills and water.

He shook his head. 'This boy will not live.'

'I believe he will. I have given him a strong dose. Would you hold the lantern? I must write the medicines that I have given on the cards they have round their necks.'

I walked across to the crowded wards where the women and children were. Close behind me came the howl of a hyaena. I gripped my knobbed stick and hurried on. From behind came a voice, 'Bwana, have I not skill in imitating?'

I let out a deep breath and waved my stick in the air. 'Mboga, I nearly attacked with my most efficient knobkerrie here.' He chuckled.

'Vegetable, there are forty patients in those wards and there is much work to be done but you're not on duty,' I said.

He grinned a weary grin. 'You have been working most of the time since before dawn. Shall I permit a *Mzungu* - a European - to do more than a *Mugogo*?'

I looked down at the clipboard. 'My special job, and I will appreciate your help in doing it, is to see that the pills are given to the right people at the right time.'

Mboga nodded. 'And tonight is a difficult one. There are so many who are dangerously ill.'

We went through the routine: pills, writing on labels, water to drink, the putting in of the small rubber tubes.

The two nurses on duty were amongst those who had earlier said that they refused to help, but both of them had changed their minds. We stood out in the starlight.

'God bless you both,' I said. 'Already some of those who lie there are improving. We will save many, many lives.'

Softly one of the girls said, 'When we saw Elisha and Jason and Pastor Daniel prepared to help we had shame.'

Mboga interrupted. 'Bwana, we will now sleep, you and I, until second cock crow and then we shall return and it will be more pills, more water, more little tubes.'

The two nurses rejoined, 'And there will be those who will come to take our place after second cock crow.'

We went through the washing of the hands routine. The water-saving idea was thoroughly understood and working well.

Before dawn the alarm clock went off again. Heavy-footed I plodded to the hospital.

'Nobody is worse.' Pastor Daniel smothered a yawn. 'I shall stay while you give the pills.'

Two of the men had high temperatures. Both were given injections of quinine. The ten-year-old boy was still too weak to swallow. Again we poured medicine and fluids down his tube. The women and children's ward were in a state of misery and chaos. All we could do was to carry on with the routine.

The next week was a nightmare medically and physically. There were occasional snatches of sleep. There were some times when we seemed to surface and relax. Recovery in people who seemed certain to die did much to encourage the staff. Often we needed to battle, especially when tiny children had to be given fluids into a vein with our primitive apparatus. What a tremendous help it would have been to have some rolls of sticking plaster.

People by the score came in. Yona and the old truck came and went. When we saw a cloud of dust growing larger along the road at the bottom of the hill urgent efforts were made to find space for new patients. Those who were convalescing slept on the verandah. Two people died.

Vaguely I remember being told, 'Bwana, there is only one tin of pills left.' My thoughts turned to the one who had stolen them.

'Where is Maradadi?' I asked.

'He has gone south along the road. Someone saw him in a lorry loaded with sheep and goats going towards Kongwa where he will sell them and make big profits.'

'Any news of Daudi?'

They shook their heads. But Elisha told me later that Daudi was working with Maradadi and selling meat to the peanut growers at Kongwa. 'He makes much money and uses it in wild ways,' he said as he tilted back his red fez.

16
Scientific Charm

At the hospital people were getting better. There was great confidence in the sulpha drugs. From time to time drastically ill people were carried in from way out in the thorn bush jungle. Yona went from village to village but he took back with him more people who had recovered than he brought in sick ones.

I finished dealing with a group of sick men who had arrived earlier that morning. I had been called urgently at midnight and here it was midday. It was a battle to keep my eyelids open.

Sechelela came over to me. 'I am not speaking now to the Bwana Doctor of the hospital. You call me grandmother and I am talking to you as I would to a grandson. Now listen,' she was smiling but serious, 'you are so busy with this wretched disease and you sleep so little that you walk round not noticing things. Keep doing this and you will be the next one to be sick.'

I could only blink at her.

'You don't realise that Bibi is too sick to work. She has a high fever and needs special treatment - not just swallowing quinine pills.'

My eyes were now wide open. 'I'll go and see her at once.'

'Before you go, do you realise that one of the water carriers has dysentery? It's better for you to know this than to have Jason worrying you. You do not realise the great value of the things that Pastor Daniel and Elisha and the schoolgirls and others from the village are doing. They work without fuss. You see Yona driving that lorry and coming with sick people but you do not hear him singing to the people in the wards, nor the girls that sing with him. Many learn the words of God because of this but you have your stethoscope in your ears. You listen to the roar of primus stoves and walk around the place like someone who has been hit on the head.'

I put my hands on her shoulders. 'Grandmother, your words are heard, but first I will deal with Bibi.'

The Australian nurse had severe malarial fever and I had to take radical steps to deal with it. Some time later I walked back to the hospital. Music came from the verandah. All who could sit up were sitting up. The mattresses were put out in the sun.

Jason was busy spraying the rubber sheeting with antiseptics. 'See, Bwana, I am using the second-hand water. Behold, does it not run into the deep hole and this medicine that kills dudus will help down there.'

'Well done, Bwana Malenga. This morning I had to treat Mhano, the water carrier, for this dysentery trouble. Will we not be short?'

The mason's eyes twinkled. 'Bwana, did you or did you not put me in charge of the water supply?'

'I did, Jason. I did indeed.'

'Well, Bwana, I called his brother to take over his work. He is a man of strength and works well. There is enough water.'

Yakobo and Mboga were hurrying towards me. 'Bwana, come and looked down the microscope. Bibi's blood slide will cause you much concern.'

The microscope showed up not only malaria but the minute corkscrew-like creatures which caused tick fever.

'I need to keep a close watch on her. Will you and Yakobo look after the giving out of medicines at sunset and midnight?'

'We will do it, Bwana,' they said both together.

With Sechelela I went to see Bibi. Her temperature was uncomfortably high. Treating malaria and tick fever was no easy matter. All three of us were relieved when the most effective medicine was safely injected.

'Good stuff, that,' murmured the sick nurse.

'Marvellous,' I agreed.

Sechelela went with me to the door. 'I shall see that Bibi is looked after, and you go and sleep with strength. I shall wake you if I need you.'

I had a double ration of water in my shower, crept under the mosquito net, tucked it in and was asleep at once. There was an insistent knocking on the door and Mboga's loud voice,  '*Hodi*, Bwana. The hospital needs you.'

I staggered out of bed sleepily. 'What's up, Mboga? What has happened?' I was struggling into my clothes.

Chuckles came from outside my window. 'First cock crow is past. Second cock crow is past. Dawn has come and gone. You have slept for nearly 12 hours.'

I yawned. 'What about the sunrise pills?'

Again that chuckle. 'They have all been given. Sechelela says, "Three babies born during the night. No trouble. Also Bibi's temperature is down to normal".'

'Spinach, I have an important job for you. I will shower and we'll have some breakfast.'

'*Yoh*! It is not the custom of this part of Africa to eat before midday.'

I called from the bathroom, 'It won't do you any harm. Get that kettle boiling.' As we ate and drank together I asked, 'What is the news?'

'The news is good. Those who gave us much trouble amongst the staff have ceased to since Hefsi went. The schoolgirls have done much work in the villages. There must be thousands of dead flies all over the countryside because of their work. Also the ways of hygiene are talked about and in many places followed.'

He stirred his cup of tea. 'Pastor Daniel spends much time among the patients telling them about Jesus. Yona sings and makes music. Also he learns much from the words of the pastor. Young Mfupi and his friend Pungu have done work that few others would agree to do.'

He drank deeply and looked hopefully at the teapot. I filled his cup again and he spooned sugar into it.

A deep voice came from the doorway. '*Hodi*, Bwana!'

I went to the door. '*Karibu*, welcome.'

'I am Mzee,' said the old man who leaned on his spear. 'I come from the village of Bogolo.' This I knew was some hundred kilometres away. 'I have seen the ways of your medicine. There are those who tell me you have medicine of great strength here.'

'That is true. But Mzee, this is the time when I *pima* - examine - the sick ones and give out medicine. Sit in the shade and when my work is finished we will talk.'

He nodded. 'It is a good word, Bwana. That I will do.'

I went over to see Bibi. She was improving slowly. 'This tick fever is no joke,' I told her. 'I'm afraid you're going to be a convalescent for quite a time. Once we get your temperature down and build a bit of strength into you we'll send you away for a holiday.'

'But...' she protested.

I held up my hand. 'What would you be telling me if I had severe malaria and tick fever on top of it?'

She smiled wearily.

'Cheer up. Things are much better at the hospital. The staff are pulling their weight and the worst of the epidemic is over. Take things quietly. Sechelela will keep an eye on you. Call me if you need anything special.'

I went on to the hospital and did the rounds. People whose lives were in danger a few days earlier were sitting outside in the sun. Under Perisi's watchful eye Jason had all the mattresses and rubber sheeting out in the sun and was using half an oil drum of 'second-hand' water to spray the walls and floor of the ward. Elisha and his two assistants were at work repairing the roof that the whirlwind had torn apart.

The old man, Mzee, stood in the shade of the pepper tree leaning on his spear. I brought two three-legged stools across, gave him one and said, '*Karibu*, welcome. You wished to talk with me.'

'*Eheh*, Bwana doctor, I have come to see the ways of your medicine that I may tell the people of my village.'

'But why come these days? Have you not heard of the great sickness which brings danger to people?'

The old man chuckled. 'Behold, Bwana, I have no fear of this disease.' His hand automatically went under the red-ochre piece of calico which, knotted over his shoulder, was his one and only garment.

I knew that somewhere about his person he wore a charm in the certain belief that it would protect him, otherwise he would not have paid a witchdoctor a goat or even a cow for it.

He leaned forward. 'In the days when I was a child this disease came upon our country. Those were the days of a famous medicine man. He had strong medicine indeed. *Koh*! I was given a *bakuli* - a dish, full of it. My father paid a cow for it. Behold, Muganga had to travel far to find the herbs and dig the roots that he put into that medicine.'

'And did you take it, Mzee?'

'Oh yes, I took it indeed. And *heeeh*, was I sick! My stomach jumped. How it jumped!'

We were silent while he took a pinch of snuff then I explained. 'These days, Mzee, we have different ways of treating troubles like this. We know that it is caused by small *dudus* - germs. If you have the medicine that kills the germs then, behold, all is well.'

'*Hongo*!' The old man raised his eyebrows. 'What a strange thing to do.'

'These are words of truth, Great One, but there is more. While the sick one is getting better he needs other medicines to give him strength. Behold, see that large bottle? That is medicine that gives strength.'

'And these smaller ones?' Mzee poked his spear towards some bottles of pills.

'These kill the *dudus* that cause trouble.'

The old man's eyes opened wide and he stood to his feet. '*Yoh*, Bwana. Those?' His amazement was beyond words. 'Show them to me. Put them into my hand that I may see them.'

I poured four of them into his hand. He carefully turned them over and looked at each side then slowly gave them back to me. Gradually a smile spread across his face. He pulled aside his cloth and there was a necklet of string tied to a small gourd, corked by a shaped thigh bone of a chicken. From this gourd he produced just such a pill as I had in my hand.

'Bwana,' he said proudly, 'I paid two goats for that. The one who sold it to me told me it was a special charm that would take all the teeth from this disease so that it could not bite me.'

I raised my eyebrows. '*Hongo*! What did he look like this one who sold you this special charm?'

'Bwana, he was a young man who wore strange clothes with many colours like the feathers of *kasuku*-the parrot.'

'And has he many goats these days because of the charms which are so strong to help people?'

The old man nodded slowly.

'Listen, Great One, those pills were stolen from me. Wear them round your middle and they're useless but swallow enough of them and the trouble loses its teeth. Outside they're useless. Inside, *hongo*! How well they work.'

Suddenly the old man laughed. 'Bwana, I have been deceived. But behold, I have another charm which is stronger still. This is the charm of the *Wachristo* - the Christians. This has special power. Behold,' he undid a bag with a purse-string top and from it produced a New Testament in Swahili. '*Koh*, Bwana, no harm can come to me while I have *kitabu* - the book, with me.'

'*Kah*, you can read?'

He shook his head. 'But, Bwana, the book is mine

and I carry it with me and no harm shall ever come my way while I carry the book of God, a holy book.'

'Great One, listen to my riddle. Suppose a man goes on safari to the dry places. Does he travel with a gourd of water slung round his shoulder? Does he say, "Behold, there is water in my gourd. I shall have no thirst"? The sun is hot, his tongue dries and he laughs. "Thirst cannot touch me. There is water in my gourd."'

'*Yoh*,' said the old man. 'If he leaves it there he will have thirst.'

'What does he do, then?'

'When thirst comes upon him he puts the gourd to his mouth and drinks.'

'Mzee, that is the word of wisdom. He drinks. What would you think of a man who went on safari and carried his gourd of water if he says "I will never thirst for, behold, I have a gourd of water"?'

Mzee shook his head. 'He is *mjinga* - a fool. If he did not put his lips to the gourd how would his thirst be stopped? What matters is water in the mouth, not merely water in a bottle.'

'And how will a man find the ways of God unless he reads what is in the book? Behold, the way you live is not the way of wisdom. This book…' I flicked over the pages, 'tells the way to be free from fear, how to be forgiven for the evil that you have done. Is not your life full of fear? You wear charms round your neck, your ankles, your middle. You even swallow charms.'

Mzee looked uneasy but said nothing.

'Behold, follow the way of wisdom, the ways of God. Come to hospital and listen as we explain them and as we tell you God's way and about his Son, Jesus. There is no deception, no trick, in the ways of God.'

Pepetua called to me. 'Bwana, we have a sick one who needs your help.'

'I must go, Great One. There is much work in this place of healing. *Kwaheri.*'

'*Kwaheri*, Bwana. We will see one another again.'

It was almost sundown when I came out of the ward and there was Mzee, waiting, leaning on his spear as I had seen him earlier in the day.

'Bwana, I have heard that the one who sold me the medicine, the one who wears the coloured clothes, has been to this village too. *Heeh*, he is a bad one.'

'You speak the truth. I know. Does he not smoke the plant we call bhang or hash-hish, which twists his wisdom and causes him to have great anger.'

At that moment young Pungu rushed through the gate. 'Bwana,' he gasped, 'a dreadful thing has happened. Ngoma bought a cigarette from Maradadi. He lost his wisdom. In great anger he...' the boy rubbed his hand over his eyes in a bewildered fashion. 'They gave me one puff. My head reels. I see things double. I...' He swayed and would have fallen had I not jumped forward and caught him.

17
Gates

The steriliser was bubbling busily on top of the primus stove. I was sharpening hypodermic needles.

Sechelela watched with interest. 'Bwana, those needles grow shorter and shorter. Are they long enough to do the work?'

'Yes, Seche. It's better for them to be short and sharp than to be long and pointed like a fish hook.'

'*Eheh*,' she agreed, 'I object to needles being stuck into me but behold they bring help that would come no other way. Have you many more to do?'

'Yes, there are still fifteen.'

She came with me as I did my rounds. Patient after patient made no protest as the needle was pushed home. Many were too ill to bother. Again the steriliser came into use and I put the syringes and needles away.

In a bed not far from the doorway was a little girl, her eyes and cheeks sunken in. Her legs looked like broomsticks.

Sechelela shook her head. 'She has been delirious all the morning.'

'Who is she?'

'She comes from a village on the far side of the swamp. Her parents are dead. She lives with some relations. They call her *Mwanda* - the slave, and that is how they treat her. If she dies they will shrug their shoulders and say, "Behold, it was the work of the ancestors. They knew how useless she was."'

'*Hongo*, she looks a nice little person.'

The child's eyes opened. She looked up at me. 'Bwana, I'm thirsty.' I held a cup of water to her lips. 'Bwana,' she asked, 'do you remember the day when you came to the village and there was singing?'

'*Eheh*, I remember. What was it that we sang that you have kept in your mind?'

'You sang about the gates of heaven. As I have been lying here I have seen them, Bwana.'

Yona had come in and was standing behind me. I held the cup of water to her lips again. She looked at Yona and said, 'It was he who sang the words. Ask him to do it again.'

'What were they, Mwanda?'

'*Kumbe*, Bwana, I know them. Does it not say there is a beautiful city over there? The gates are shut to evil, though, and no kind of sin will ever enter in.' As she spoke Yona started to sing quietly.

I looked at the label round the child's neck and measured out the pills that she should take. 'Take these, Mwanda. They will give you strength.'

She shook her head. '*Ng'o* - No - Bwana. Do not

give them to me. Use them on someone else.' Her voice had dropped to a whisper.

I bent over the cot. 'Take them, child. They'll give you strength so that you may again walk and talk and play with your companions.'

'*Kah*, Bwana, there is no play in my life. For many days my leg has no strength. This has been so ever since they burnt me with a stick from the fire. It was a thing of wonder. The glowing red of the stick burnt my skin but there was no pain.'

There was an ugly ulcer on her leg and, looking at it, I found what was all too common in our part of Africa. She had leprosy.

'Come, Mwanda, take your pills. They will help you.'

She swallowed them and then smiled. 'I have had joy today, Bwana. I have stood before the gates.'

'*Hongo*,' said Sechelela. 'Have you no fear?'

There was amazement written all over Mwanda's face. 'Fear? But, Bwana, these gates I've been looking through are not the gates of death, they are the gates to heaven. There is much difference. Behold, is he not there? Bwana, when you spoke words that day at our village did you not tell us of Jesus and tell us to ask him to take from our lives the evil that stops us from entering through the gate? You said if we did he would forgive and when he has done so does he not stand there to welcome us? Have I not asked him to do this? Why then should I fear? What is there to be afraid of?' She closed her eyes. 'I would sleep now.'

There was the sound of a four-wheel-drive machine

pulling up outside the hospital gate. Mfupi came running towards me. 'Bwana, there is a policeman, one whom we helped at the hospital last year. He has come to greet you.'

I went out to shake hands with the Inspector of Police, a tall and impressive man.

He said, 'I'm afraid I have bad news for you. One of your young men - he was actually in the football team that played against the police six months or so ago - is in serious trouble. It appears he's been smoking hash-hish and as you know it often makes people unstable. This happened with young Ngoma. In his frenzy he killed one of the men who was with him with a knobbed stick. I've just arrested Ngoma. Things look bad.'

'Where did this happen, Bwana Inspector?'

'Over there,' said the policeman indicating the village where Maradadi had last been seen.

'Did you, by any chance, hear that a stranger had visited the place dressed in the brightest of clothes?'

'Yes, he was there and my informers tell me that he behaved in strange ways but I have nothing against him. Why?'

'I would think he is the one who caused all this trouble. He is the one who has brought hash-hish into this part of the country, even to the hospital itself.'

'Have you any evidence?'

'Yes. A boy came in only last night wanting to tell me of some dreadful event. Before he could tell me what it was he collapsed and went into a fit from the effects of smoking a marijuana cigarette.'

'But you can't prove that this Maradadi gave it to him?'

'You're right, but you should be able to get some clear information from the young man you've arrested.' The policeman nodded slowly. 'It's a tragic thing about Ngoma,' I went on. 'I only wish you had grabbed this Maradadi a week ago. Even now if you could get your hands on him you'd be doing something worthwhile. He stole a considerable number of sulpha pills that are the spearhead of my battle for the lives of people in the hospital. We have witnesses to prove he did that.'

'Are you in trouble with these pills?'

'We look like being short of them before the epidemic is over.'

I went across to the car where, sitting between *askaris*, was a young, well-educated twenty-year-old whose life I had watched with interest. He was full of potential but unfortunately had a pride that could be played up to by anybody. Maradadi had found this out and by a lot of smooth talk had persuaded him to smoke marijuana. There was my young friend looking befuddled, gesticulating violently with his right hand, the hand that only a few hours before had taken the life of his best friend.

The inspector put his hand on my shoulder. 'It's a nasty business, especially after all that you've done for this fellow.'

Before I could reply Mboga hurried to me. 'Bwana, quickly. Come to the ward. Mwanda is asking for you.'

I turned to the policeman. 'Would you care to come and see the other side of our job?'

We walked quickly together picking our way through the patients who were lying on the floor on mats. We came to Mwanda's cot.

In a surprisingly clear voice she said, 'Bwana, the gate is opening and I can see him. He stands there and welcomes me. I have no fear now. I am passing through the gate. Tell the others that there is no fear when you come to the gates of heaven and you love Jesus. Tell them, Bwana.' She sank back on her pillow.

My fingers went to her wrist. There was no pulse.

The inspector was standing behind me. He said huskily, 'I wish I knew what that child knows.'

He strode off and I watched his car, carrying tragedy in it, disappear into the heat haze of an East African afternoon.

18
Cramp

Yakobo was busy working with the microscope.

'Have you heard whether Baruti, the hunter, is anywhere near these days?'

'*Eheh*, I saw him in the village.'

'Would you send someone to find him because those who are recovering from dysentery have small strength in their bodies. We should give them proteins.'

'*Yoh*, Bwana. I hear many times the words proteins and fats and carbohydrates. Fats I understand and carbohydrates.' He rolled his eyes. 'Bwana, are they not in porridge and sugar? But proteins?'

'Protein is the stuff which helps you to repair damage in your muscles. It's important for growth and for healing. You find it in milk and meat and fish and quite a lot in eggs. I want Baruti to go round the villages and get all the eggs and milk that he can. Give him a large bag of sugar and he can exchange sugar for protein - milk and eggs and, if possible, meat.'

Yakobo's eyes twinkled. 'Tell him to be careful about the eggs. See that each one is placed in water. If it stays on the bottom he takes it. If it floats…' Yakobo wrinkled up his nose and lifted his eyebrows.

A nurse came running towards me. 'Quickly, Bwana. Trouble. Great pain.' I followed her to where a woman lay, her face twisted in agony.

'*Eeeeh*,' she groaned. '*Eeeeh*.' Her voice rose to a scream.

I could see the muscles of her legs were bunched up. She had an acute cramp. 'Push,' I urged as I forced the palm of my hand against her foot. 'Push your heel down. Hard!' She pushed and her face relaxed. '*Yoh*! *Yoh*! The pain of it.' She clutched the side of the bed.

I turned to the nurse. 'Pep, do what I'm doing. Push against her foot. See that she stretches it out. We need medicine that will get at the cause of these cramps.'

A husky whisper came from across the ward. '*Yoh*… I have fear. This is the work of *mapepo* - spirits. See how it claws at her muscles.'

'You are deceived!' I spoke forcefully. 'This is not the work of a devil as you think. Behold, in these days of her sickness she has lost much salt from her body. Has she not sweated and sweated?'

I turned to the woman who was pushing hard against Pepetua's hand. 'It is so, Bwana. Every night, *yoh*! It was as though I had been standing in the rain.'

'Right. Now keep pushing. I'll be with you in a minute.'

In the hospital kitchen I picked up a lump of crude salt and a handful of freshly cooked *ugali*. I mixed the two together and rolled them into pills about half the size of a marble, put them in a piece of gourd and ran back to where the woman was in a near frenzy and Pepetua was doing all she knew how to keep the cramped leg out straight.

Suddenly the cramp gripped the other leg. She was so intent in voicing her misery that she took no notice of the pills I had made. 'Come now,' I coaxed. 'Take these. They will stop your pain. Chew them up and swallow them.'

She crammed six of my home made anti-cramp pellets into her mouth.

'*Yoh*,' she gasped, 'they're salty.'

'Truly, and it's salt that's doing the work. In those pills there's nothing but salt and porridge. Now drink water and plenty of it.'

She drank deeply. '*Kah*!' Her voice was full of disgust. 'That will do me no good.'

Anxious eyes watched her from every corner of the ward. Pepetua had put her legs back onto the bed and covered them up.

The woman gasped, '*Yoh*! There's another one coming.'

'Stretch out your heel,' ordered the nurse.

The woman did so and surprise crept over her face. '*Koh*, that one did not have the same strength as the others.'

Half an hour later I heard an enthusiastic report from Pepetua. 'Bwana, that is medicine. That was a thing that brought understanding to the people of the ward. Salt they know and porridge they know and sweat they know and understand. It is clearly in their minds now why cramps occur. They say that, truly, this is a way of wisdom. *Koh*, to think that salt would do all that.'

On the windowsill was a New Testament in the Chigogo language. 'Pep, open God's book at St Matthew, chapter 5, verse 13. See what it says.'

The girl thumbed through the pages and read, 'You are the salt of the earth. If salt loses its taste what is there left to give taste to it? There's no more to be done to it but to throw it out of the door for people to tread underfoot.'

Pepetua nodded. 'These are true words, Bwana. Behold, if there is no taste in salt why put it into porridge?'

'*Eheh*, and if you put it into pills like those pills there they would not relieve cramp.'

'*Kumbe*!' The nurse sounded puzzled. 'Bwana, what does it all mean?'

'Jesus spoke these words about salt. He is speaking of the people who belong to him, who are members of his family - not people who merely call themselves Christians. That sort of person is like salt with no taste. They're not fit for anything and they do nothing useful in life. The only Christians whose lives are a joy to God are the ones whose lives have taste about them. That taste speaks of usefulness, of kindness, of love. That taste comes in two main ways.'

'What are they, doctor?'

'Behold, when a person talks to God - not just sometimes but often - his life becomes salty, salty in the way that Jesus spoke of. And also when a person reads the words of God, reads them and does what they say, this puts taste into life.'

Pepetua rolled her eyes. 'These are words of difficulty.'

'Not really. Have you ever watched a woman weaving mats?'

She nodded. 'I, too, can weave.'

'Well think of God's words as coloured threads. Weave them into your life. That makes you salty.'

She was thoughtful for a time then she pointed with her chin towards the sick woman. 'Behold, salt with a tang works. Look at her now.'

Our patient was sitting up in bed looking an entirely different person. '*Yoh*, Bwana, there was strength in that medicine. Not only has my pain gone but I feel better!'

As I came back from giving the pills at sunset I went past the kitchen and saw Pepetua talking enthusiastically to a lot of people about salt. Sitting on wooden stool in a corner was Baruti. He got to his feet and came across. '*Mbwuka*, Bwana.'

I took him firmly by the hand. '*Mbwuka*, Baruti. What is the news of many days?'

'The news is good. I have brought many eggs and much milk will be coming in tomorrow.' He took me by the arm and led me outside. 'Also, Bwana, I have news of Maradadi.'

'What's he been up to now?'

'Behold, he is *manumit* - an evil one. Did he not cause hot anger and have a fierce quarrel with the chief of the town called Hulabit? Behold...'

Baruti went on to tell a story which was full to the brim of viciousness. Baruti paused. 'The chief had fierce anger. He called for his armed guard and ordered that Maradadi be given ten lashes with a hippo-hide whip. Maradadi screamed and cursed then he went to the *kaya* where he was living and beat his woman companion till she fell to the ground and fainted.'

'*Kumbe*, Baruti. Did nobody attempt to stop him?'

'It was too late. When the people did come his evil work was over. And, Bwana, you know the girl. Was she not a nurse at this hospital? Is her name not Hefsi?'

'*Hongo*, poor Hefsi. She didn't deserve that.'

Baruti shook his head. 'When I saw how ill she looked I arranged with the chief that she be carried into the hospital. She will be arriving not long after *Mbisi*, the hyaena, starts his evening song.'

As if taking up the challenge, from the thorn bush behind the hospital came the long drawn, mournful cry of a hyaena.

'*Yoh*,' shuddered Pepetua. 'Behold, that is an evil song.'

Baruti grinned and held a spear in his capable hand. 'Heeh, it is indeed. But do not have fear'. He paused...'Although there are strange things happening these days.'

19

Ominous Night

'Sechelela,' I asked, 'share your wisdom with me. Where can we put a bed for Hefsi? We can't put her in the ward where all the mothers and babies are. We can't put her in with all the people who have dysentery. We'll have to fit her in somewhere.'

The head nurse considered carefully. 'Baruti's words make me think she has great pain and will need medicine from a syringe to ease her pain. Why not put a stretcher in the store where we keep the blankets and the soap and the kerosene?'

'That is a word of wisdom, grandmother.'

Seche was shaking her head. 'Poor girl. She has suffered but did we not warn her? Did we not tell her with words that had no anger in them that if you sow the wind you reap the whirlwind? And behold, she is paying - how much we will know before long, but everything is ready. The cooking is finished. Come and eat *ugali* with us round the camp fire. Baruti is here and also Yona. There will be stories and singing.'

Mboga brought me a three-legged stool and Pepetua a kettle and a bucket. She poured water over my hands, my right held above my left, the bucket in place so that none would be wasted.

Yona came close to me. 'I hear that you have skill eating food like we do.'

'*Eheh*, Yona. I eat with joy but…' I shook my head. 'You will hear the voice of the snake within me.'

There was a gust of approving laughter showing that I had used the right words to describe belching.

Steaming bowls of porridge were brought. Mboga stood up. 'Let us thank God for our food.' He did so and then passed the dish of porridge to me. I moulded a lump in my right hand, shaped it like a small doughnut and dipped it into a dish containing green jelly-like 'relish'. They watched carefully as I put it into my mouth.

Sechelela chuckled. 'He has learned his lessons well.'

For a time there was little talk. The porridge was dealt with enthusiastically. At last Yona stood up. '*Yoh*,' he said, stroking his middle. '*Nghwiguta* - I have no more room.' Then he started to sing. There was laughter from all sides.

When he had finished I asked, 'Yona, what do all those words mean? I could only make out half of it.'

'They're merely words, Bwana. I don't know what they mean myself. It's the right sort of song to sing at this time after a meal round the camp fire when stories are going to be told. Everyone ought to join in the chorus.'

'*Eheh*, I know the sort of thing. We have one in our language which says a lot of things that have little meaning. Then all join together "singing polly wolly doodle all the day".'

'*Heeh*,' said Yona, 'you must teach me that song, Bwana.'

'I will do that, but, first, sing me something else, something that is closer to your heart.'

He answered with a nod. 'I know what you mean…' He began, ' "I will not stop singing".' When he finished the last line, On the cross he died that I might be forgiven, he said, 'Oh yes, that is the song closest to my heart, Bwana.'

At that moment, walking along the hospital verandah came what the staff called Mpussi, the hospital cat, which dealt so effectively with quite a number of things on four legs and sometimes with snakes.

'*Heeh*,' said Sechelela. 'Look at her.'

The cat stopped about a metre outside the near circle of light. Her tail moved restlessly to and fro. Baruti was on his feet. 'Behold, Mpussi has fear in her heart.'

Sala scrambled to her feet and let out the piercing danger cry. Mingled with it came an almost human scream from the cat as, like a flash out of the shadows, streaked the ugly shape of a hyaena. It seized the cat in its jaws and disappeared into the darkness. The whole thing was over in a flash. Baruti picked up his spear and dashed in the direction of the hospital gate but he did not even see the hyaena. Some minutes later, out in the thorn bush we heard its snarling voice. It seemed raised in derision.

At the other side of the hospital grounds I could see a twinkle of light. I shuddered. 'This is an evil night. Who is coming over there?'

The light came closer and soon we saw a messenger who held out an envelope addressed with one word: *Doctor.* I tore it open. Written in English was the message:

Hefsi has tasted the teeth of the whip. She is now tasting the medicine of the tribe. My thoughts tell me that the Bwana is a fool. Let him find medicine if he can to overcome the strength of the spell which will be cast.

I jumped to my feet. 'Tell me. Who was the sender of this letter?'

The messenger tilted back the red fez on his head, spat on the ground and made an insulting gesture as he stalked out of the firelight. As I moved towards him he broke into a run, turning his head to shriek a final insult. To his obvious shock he ran straight into the strong arms of the hunter who dragged him into the firelight.

'*Yoh!*' came Baruti's deep resonant voice. 'Two hyenas travel the same path, eh? What were the words I heard you say to the Bwana? Behold, you shall swallow them. You shall swallow them with strength.'

'Put him down, Baruti,' I said and, turning to the messenger, 'Who wrote that letter?'

'*Magu*, Bwana, I don't know.'

'Heh!' growled Baruti. 'Your memory had better work.'

The messenger cowered from the menace of the hunter's spear. 'Come,' I ordered sternly, 'Who was it?'

'Don't let him hurt me. It was a man wearing a yellow shirt and purple trousers and red socks. Truly, Bwana.'

'He sent it to me, did he? Where did you see him?'

'Bwana, it was at the village of Chibaya. He came up with those who carried Hefsi in a hammock. He gave them shillings and told them to return to their homes and leave her under a buyu tree. He also gave me shillings and told me to give this letter to you.'

'Did he tell you how to give it?'

The messenger, now thoroughly frightened, whined, 'Bwana, it is his work, not mine.'

'Mboga, Baruti and Yona, will you come with me? We must get hold of this girl before something worse happens to her.'

'One thing first,' said Baruti. 'What shall I do with this jackal?' He prodded Maradadi's messenger with the blunt end of his spear.

'I have no interest in him. Come quickly, Baruti. Let's go.'

We moved off towards the truck. Every minute was valuable. Baruti lingered behind and pitched the messenger's hat high into the air for it to fall among a tangle of thorn bush and I heard him shout, 'Mbisi has just carried a cat to its death. Remember that hyaenas will eat any sort of filth, even their own kind, so be careful.'

Twice during that drive through the darkness hyaenas slunk through the beam of the headlights. '*Yoh*, Bwana, this night is an evil one,' muttered Mboga.

Some distance from the village of Chibaya beside a small fire lay Hefsi. An old African crone spat and hobbled off as we pulled up. Nobody answered as I called greetings to the people of the village. Nobody appeared.

I bent over the girl. She cowered back in fear. 'Bwana, don't strike me.'

'It's not our way to do this sort of thing, Hefsi. We've come to help. Behold, you have sorrow of heart and pain tortures your body. Shall we not help you?'

She groaned as we prepared to lift her into the truck. 'Bwana,' she gasped, 'He beat me. That was bad but *yoh*! Other pains came upon me, great pains and, *heh*! they brought me to this village and left me here. Fears of death came. Bwana, my child was born. It was too small to live and the old women have told me that I will die also.'

20
Reaping The Whirlwind

But Hefsi did not die. In silent despair she lay, scarcely eating a thing. Then, one night, she disappeared.

At dawn Elisha called, '*Hodi*' at my window. 'Bwana, Hefsi has run away and there is great fear at the hospital. At first cock crow a man wrapped in a black cloth cast a strong spell. There is the cunning of Maradadi behind this.'

As we talked together I had the feeling, although I could see nobody, that there were a lot of people watching my every action. I had had the same feeling when there had been a cobra loose in the linen cupboard. Now, a cobra is not the sort of creature I like to handle under any circumstances. I would much rather tackle a spell, even a strong one.

Elisha went on, 'Bwana, come with me to the kitchen. I will show you this thing which produces fear in the hearts of sick ones and even of the nurses.'

I expected something grim and gruesome, but

there across the entrance to the kitchen was a string of white enamel plates with what looked like ashes on them. You couldn't step through the doorway without treading on one. All the way to the flour bin, to the baskets, to the pounding mortars and the other pots and gourds that the girls used in preparing and cooking *ugali* was this long chain of enamel plates.

I went across and looked at them closely. I could see people peering from behind trees. Others were in nearby doorways. All stood in silence watching what I would do. I found it hard not to regard this as a practical joke but the scared expressions of those who watched made it clear that this was no ordinary matter.

Softly I asked , 'Elisha, how do you deal with a charm like this?'

'If someone had the courage to wash those plates the charm would lose its strength.'

'If I wash them would that take the strength from the spell?'

He nodded and for a moment hesitated. 'And I will help you, Bwana.'

I put my hands on his shoulders. 'That gives me joy. But tell me. Enamel plates seem a most ordinary sort of spell to me. Why not use gourds or cooking pots, something particularly African, not ordinary enamel plates?' I picked one up and turned it over. 'And made in China at that!'

The corners of Elisha's mouth twitched. He called out, 'Please bring some hot water.'

A girl reappeared quickly with half a kerosene tin full. Behind her another nurse came with a tin dish. Elisha and I picked up plates, put them in the hot water and washed them. We stacked them and then I took the dish of water and poured it into the deep hole. People had come out into the sunlight and were watching with interest.

I called one of the junior nurses, 'Would you put these back in the store, please?'

She didn't hesitate and carried the plates back to their normal shelf. A sigh of relief seemed to echo round the hospital.

I spoke loudly, '*Yoh!* What a charm. Who could have planned this but Maradadi?'

'*Eheh*,' agreed Sechelela. 'But, Bwana, you don't realise how much this sort of thing brings fear to people, especially those who are not members of God's tribe.' Turning to all those who clustered round she said, 'It is a thing of true wisdom to trust God. He is of great strength and can at all times overcome the cunning of *shaitan* - the devil.' She paused. 'Who fears hyaena when lion is his friend?'

'Seche, you speak words of wisdom. It says clearly in the Bible, "Resist the devil and he will run away from you. Come close to God and he will come close to you."'

'*Hongo*,' said Mboga, 'this is true, Bwana, but going God's way is not a smooth path. And *yoh!* Look at this Maradadi. He seems to have got away with everything so far and, behold, do you not remember right at the beginning you spoke about him: the day when *ifulafumbi* - the whirlwind, attacked us. Did you not say that those who sow the wind will reap a harvest of whirlwinds?'

'*Hongo,*' said Elisha. 'Bwana, behold, Maradadi has received no harvest as yet.'

'*Hodi,*' called Mboga.

'Welcome,' I said, 'What is the news?'

In English he replied, 'The news is not good. Mfupi has the disease with strength. It struck him in the middle of the night and even now he has the look that we have learnt to fear.'

'We need to get him into hospital fast, then. Will you ask Yona to bring him in?'

'It is already being done, Bwana.'

'Excellent. And, Mboga, I have had a letter telling me we cannot expect any more sulpha pills for at least a month. We'd better check our stock.'

I heard the old truck grinding its way up the hill as Mboga ran in. 'Report on pills, Bwana. When we have treated the people who are still sick in hospital there are only thirty left.'

These words rang through my mind as I looked down at the sick boy. At this same time yesterday I had been talking to a normal, well-nourished boy. Now he was gaunt, barely conscious and his skin burned with fever.

'Eight pills at once, Mboga.'

'Will we need to put the small tube into his stomach, Bwana?'

'I'm afraid so. He's too sick to swallow. I will also have to run fluids into a vein in his arm. To save him we must work fast and use every weapon we have.'

We worked together and, in the early afternoon, there was a deep sense of relief in the hospital when Mfupi was able to chew up his second lot of pills and swallow them. Then it became clear that he had malaria as well and it was not till three days later that his temperature was normal and he was able to take reasonable nourishment.

'Three more pills left,' said Pepetua, 'and he still needs exactly that number.'

Elisha came to the window. 'The roof is now fixed, Bwana, and the beams mended.'

'That's splendid. I have been reviewing the results of this dysentery epidemic. We have had eighty-two people in hospital. Only two have died whereas before...' I looked questioningly at Elisha.

'*Koh*, Bwana, people died, scores of them, all over the country.'

'What a good thing it is that no new sick ones have come in. With Maradadi stealing all those sulpha pills of ours we could be facing tragedy again and again.'

For two days Mfupi was in trouble but on the third, as I arrived to do ward rounds, I saw him sitting out in the sun.

'*Mbwuka*, Bwana. I am better today. I have only two more pills to take.'

'This is a thing of joy, Mfupi. There's great value in those pills. When dysentery attacked you we were at the very end of our stock. God was good to you.' The boy nodded quietly.

At last I felt a lifting of the stress of the last tumultuous weeks.

Mboga felt it too. 'Bwana, *heeeh*, the burden is off my shoulders. I...'

'You speak too soon, Spinach. Look.'

Coming towards us through the late afternoon shadows were a group of people carrying a sick person. They paused at the verandah.

Their leader said, 'Bwana, we come from the village of Hakamu. We bring a man whose sickness is great. He has the disease of these days. Behold, the gates that lead to the ancestors seem close to him.'

He pointed to the man being carried in a blanket pinned in position with long thorns onto a bamboo pole. 'The medicines of the tribe are in vain. There are charms about his neck but the spell cast against him is stronger. It struck him suddenly and now his wisdom has disappeared.' He shrugged his shoulders. '*Heeh.*'

By this time the blanket had been lowered to the floor. I pulled out the thorns and there lay a young man. A rough bandage covered much of his head and a filthy bit of black cloth was round his middle. It was the usual grim picture of acute dysentery. His ribs seemed to stick out from skin dry as parchment. He was typical of the people who had been coming to us during the past hectic weeks.

I shook my head. 'We could have done a lot for this man if only we had the medicine. The strong pills we call sulpha could have helped him greatly and probably saved his life but a thief called Maradadi stole many of these and our supply is finished.'

I listened to his chest. His heart beat fast and weakly. His spleen was enlarged. I gave an injection of quinine. He certainly had malaria but it was obvious that he was one of those where dysentery had stuck like a cobra. The venom of the disease would need the strongest form of counter-attack.

Mboga and Yakobo stood on either side of me. 'Is it too late, Bwana?'

I nodded. 'We're facing a hopeless situation. This man is one whose life could have been saved. He needs a huge dose: eight or even twelve pills at once and then four more every six hours. If we had the pills we could have his sickness under control in three days but we haven't any left.'

Yakobo didn't seem to be listening. He had a moist towel in his hand and was wiping away a thick layer of red dust from the sick man's face and hair. Excitedly he exclaimed, 'Bwana, look! Look who it is! This is no ordinary man from the village. It's…'

The people who had carried the man in waited for nothing more. They took to their heels and ran.

I went to the door. '*Heeh*,' I shouted, '*Mukubita hayi* - where are you going?'

Elisha gripped my arm. 'Bwana, come, look again.

I peered down at the gaunt figure on the floor.

'Bwana,' muttered Mboga, 'don't you understand? This is Maradadi!'

There was a long pause. 'You're right,' I breathed, 'and there is nothing we can do for him. He's dying simply because we haven't got the pills that could save his life, the pills that he himself stole.'

Elisha shook his head slowly. 'Truly, he sowed the wind and this is his harvest. Is it not *ifulafumbi* - the whirlwind?'

Weeks went by.

Elisha was mending a door. He stopped with his hammer poised. '*Koh*, Bwana. I have news that is food for the ears.'

From his red fez he produced a crumpled note. 'I wrote to Daudi and told him news of the whirlwind and of Maradadi's harvest. I told him the news of his planting.' The carpenter adjusted a pair of glasses of which he was very proud.

'Daudi says, "Truly, I have sown foolishness. There is no joy in my path. My heart is sad when I think of the ways of the hospital. There is homesickness..." *Heeh*,' smiled the carpenter, 'there is much of this. His nose thirsts for the smell of ether and carbolic,' he turned the page. 'Here it is, Bwana, "I have asked forgiveness from God. My mind is changed from my old desires. My feet would follow my mind back to my work at the hospital, even if it is only scrubbing floors and washing clothes. But the Bwana, how can he forget my anger and..."'

I interrupted. '*Hongo*, Elisha, and so our prayer is answered.'

'*Kumbe*!' The carpenter scratched his head with a nail and grinned. 'It will be good to see Daudi, the old Daudi, back in our hospital.'

SAMPLE CHAPTER FROM: JUNGLE DOCTOR IN SLIPPERY PLACES

1

Unwelcome Patient

'That man Dolla is with us again,' said Doctor Daudi Matama.

Mboga laughed. 'Truly, his head is of bone. He dived through the window of the train because he thought he saw a policeman. I saw it happen. His arms held tightly to a steel box and his head struck a large stone with a heavy thump.'

'Did you use the wisdom you are taught here?'

'That and more,' chuckled Mboga. 'Is he not here in the men's ward, sewn up, bandaged, treated for shock and doing as well as can be expected? But, Dr Daudi, you should have seen his clothes – lovely colours. They will make Yakobo's eyes stick out with jealousy.'

In the ward the young doctor examined the injured man. He turned to Yakobo, the hospital's senior male nurse. 'He needs rest and quiet. Call me if his pulse rate changes.'

As he went through the door the doctor was

remembering, 'When he and that trickster Lugu were in here a year ago a change started to come over Yakobo. I only hope Dolla's present visit doesn't make things worse.'

Yakobo counted the unconscious man's pulse and noted it on his chart. He picked up the double-locked steel box, put it in a cupboard and packed Dolla's folded clothing neatly on top of it. He sighed.

From the far end of the ward a quavering voice demanded, 'Give me medicines for the snake within me.' Yakobo grunted. A small boy chose that moment to be violently sick. Yakobo groaned aloud.

Glancing at the clock he saw it was time to take Dolla's pulse again. His hand had barely touched the bandaged wrist when Dolla's one visible eye opened. There was a gleam in it.

Huskily the sick man spoke. 'There is a key in my pocket. Open the steel box and take out a parcel and a transistor radio. Hide that parcel safely and the radio is yours.'

Yakobo whispered urgently, 'Keep your voice down. Mboga is here and his ears are large.'

'So is his mouth,' hissed Dolla. 'This matter must be kept secret.'

Mboga strolled up. 'How's our tough friend?'

Yakobo shook his head, put his hand on Mboga's shoulder and tiptoed with him to the door. 'We must keep him quiet and give complete rest. Please go and tell Dr Daudi that the pulse is slower and temperature normal.'

Mboga was no sooner out of sight than Yakobo

moved to the cupboard, unlocked the box and pushed two packages up his shirt.

At midday the doctor came to the ward. Dolla was propped up, muttering and breathing fast. 'Hold him forward, Yakobo. I want to listen to his chest.' After a minute Dr Matama took his stethoscope from his ears. 'It's penicillin for him, or he'll have pneumonia on top of his head injuries.'

Yakobo nodded, went to the medicine cupboard and returned with a syringe and penicillin. He rolled up Dolla's sleeve and said in a low voice, 'Your parcel is fixed firmly under the ward table with sticking plaster. No one ever looks under there.'

'OK,' muttered Dolla.

Yakobo injected expertly.

Again Dolla's eye opened. 'You do that well. I've had many injections but none as good as that.'

Yakobo felt a warm glow inside him.

Dolla's voice came again, 'Why work here for wages that only whisper in your pocket when you could be rich and buy anything you want?'

Yakobo shrugged. 'I have told you before, there is much interest and satisfaction in the work of the hospital.'

Dolla sneered. 'You can't eat, drink or wear satisfaction and interest. Do you enjoy listening to the complaining voices of the sick or doing work that is not food for the nose? What joy you must get out of giving medicines and making beds! What satisfaction there must be in working at night when you might be sleeping or better still be in the town having fun!'

The male nurse put down the syringe. 'What are you up to, Dolla? Does it please you to disturb my mind and bring unsettling thoughts into my head?'

There was disgust in Dolla's voice. 'Disturb! Unsettle! Are you a complete fool? Doesn't your mind protest when you hear voices that order, Yakobo do this, Yakobo do that, Yakobo come here, Yakobo go there? Open your eyes, man! For merely hiding a packet you've become the owner of a powerful transistor radio. Can't you see that with enough penicillin and the skill you have you could quickly become rich, amazingly rich, in the villages and towns? Many desire medicine for the disease that is spoken of only in whispers.' His voice was high-pitched with excitement. 'There are thousands and thousands of shillings for someone like you with the right people to help him.'

'Yakobo,' called a voice urgently. 'Yakobo.'

'What was I saying?' breathed Dolla. 'If you're fool enough to keep on living this way, it's your affair.'

Yakobo turned away sharply. As he hurried down the ward he stumbled, grabbed at the syringe and missed. Mboga stood in the doorway and laughed. 'There is no joy in broken syringes. Last week I lost two shillings from my wages for doing that.'

Kicking the glass under a bed, Yakobo walked out of the ward. He glanced at the marking on the sleeve of his tunic and thought, 'After seven years' service, because I do not make trouble I'm pushed about and ordered to do this and that like a first-year trainee.'

He passed a window. Dr Matama's voice called. 'Yakobo, don't forget you have those blood specimens to examine.'

With difficulty he replied quietly, 'Yes, doctor.' His head seemed to throb with anger as he muttered under his breath, 'Dolla was right. I've something better to do than work with a microscope. I'll listen to the world on that transistor and I'll tune in to any station I want.'

Then he saw a bunch of keys in the storeroom door. One of these he knew would open the dispensary. There were riches for him in that dispensary with its bottles of penicillin and syringes and needles. He made sure no one was looking, then in a few seconds the key was off the bunch and in his pocket.

Jungle Doctor Series

Jungle Doctor and the Whirlwind
ISBN 978-1-84550-296-6

Jungle Doctor on the Hop
ISBN 978-1-84550-297-3

Jungle Doctor Spots a Leopard
ISBN 978-1-84550-301-7

Jungle Doctor's Crooked Dealings
ISBN 978-1-84550-299-7

Jungle Doctor's Enemies
ISBN 978-1-84550-300-0

Jungle Doctor in Slippery Places
ISBN 978-1-84550-298-0

Jungle Doctor's Africa
ISBN 978-1-84550-388-8

Jungle Doctor on Safari
ISBN 978-1-84550-391-8

Jungle Doctor Meets a Lion
ISBN 978-1-84550-392-5

Eyes on Jungle Doctor
ISBN 978-1-84550-393-2

Jungle Doctor Stings a Scorpion
ISBN 978-1-84550-390-1

Jungle Doctor Pulls a Leg
ISBN 978-1-84550-389-5